I0094720

DISINVENTIONS

RSA·STR

THE RSA SERIES IN TRANSDISCIPLINARY RHETORIC

Edited by
Michael Bernard-Donals (University of Wisconsin) and
Leah Ceccarelli (University of Washington)

Editorial Board:
Diane Davis, The University of Texas at Austin
Cara Finnegan, University of Illinois at Urbana-Champaign
Debra Hawhee, The Pennsylvania State University
John Lynch, University of Cincinnati
Steven Mailloux, Loyola Marymount University
Kendall Phillips, Syracuse University
Thomas Rickert, Purdue University

The RSA Series in Transdisciplinary Rhetoric is a collaboration with the Rhetoric Society of America to publish innovative and rigorously argued scholarship on the tremendous disciplinary breadth of rhetoric. Books in the series take a variety of approaches, including theoretical, historical, interpretive, critical, or ethnographic, and examine rhetorical action in a way that appeals, first, to scholars in communication studies and English or writing, and, second, to at least one other discipline or subject area.

A complete list of books in this series is located at the back of this volume.

José Manuel Cortez

DISINVENTIONS

Rhetorics of Undocumented Immigration
in the Deterrence Era

THE PENNSYLVANIA STATE UNIVERSITY PRESS
UNIVERSITY PARK, PENNSYLVANIA

Library of Congress Cataloging-in-Publication Data

Names: Cortez, José Manuel author.
Title: Disinventions : rhetorics of undocumented immigration
    in the deterrence era / José Manuel Cortez.
Description: University Park, Pennsylvania : The Pennsylvania
    State University Press, [2025] | Series: The RSA series
    in transdisciplinary rhetoric | Includes bibliographical
    references and index.
Summary: "Examines the cultural, political, and rhetorical
    effects of federal immigration practices to propose a new
    way to engage discourses of undocumented immigration.
    Highlights the non-West and colonial other as products of
    Western hegemony and colonialism, arguing that theories
    of decolonization based on hybridity privilege some at the
    expense of others"—Provided by publisher.
Identifiers: LCCN 2025017100 | ISBN 9780271100234
    hardback, 9780271100241 paperback
Subjects: LCSH: Illegal immigration—Mexican-American
    Border Region | Noncitizens—Mexican-American Border
    Region | Rhetoric—Political aspects—Mexican-American
    Border Region | Mexico—Emigration and immigration |
    United States—Emigration and immigration | United
    States—Emigration and immigration—Government policy
Classification: LCC JV6465 .C76 2025
LC record available at https://lccn.loc.gov/2025017100

Copyright © 2025 José Manuel Cortez
All rights reserved
Printed in the United States of America
Published by The Pennsylvania State University Press,
University Park, PA 16802–1003

© The Rhetoric Society of America, 2025

The Pennsylvania State University Press is a member of the
Association of University Presses.

It is the policy of The Pennsylvania State University Press to
use acid-free paper. Publications on uncoated stock satisfy the
minimum requirements of American National Standard for
Information Sciences—Permanence of Paper for Printed
Library Material, ANSI z39.48–1992.

For Dana, Finn, and Reyna:

To love without conditions, despite everything

Contents

Illustrations

Maps

Acknowledgments

This book is a seedling in the understory of an old-growth forest. *Disinventions* grew with the support of many mother trees, who collected sunlight and distributed vitamin D and other nutrients down through underground networks of mycelium into the understory where this book still grows.

Disinventions would not exist without the support of the staff at Pennsylvania State University Press. I am grateful to work with Archna Patel, who has been a brilliant and thoughtful editor. Her editorial vision has made the book stronger in every way. Thank you to Josie DiKerby and the entire production team. Karma Chávez and Christa Olson reviewed the book for the press. I express enormous appreciation for their deep and extensive feedback, which I received at a time when I really needed it. Thank you to Michael Bernard-Donals and Leah Ceccarelli, editors of the RSA Series in Transdisciplinary Rhetoric, for their generous feedback and guidance.

The seeds of *Disinventions* found soil in an Américan rhetoric seminar at the 2015 Rhetoric Society of America summer institute at the University of Wisconsin, Madison, led by Christa Olson and René de los Santos. I am indebted to René, whose work paved the way for rhetoricians of Latin America. It was there that I met Christa Olson, in whose mentorship and friendship I have found a fortune of joy.

Abraham Acosta and Maritza Cárdenas have always modeled for me a kind of deep scholarship that I aspire to write. They also mentored me through some of the most challenging moments of my life. Without their guidance, I'm sure I wouldn't have made it this far. I am grateful for their limitless care. Also supporting me from the beginning at the University of Arizona were Sonia Arellano, Adolfo Béjar Lara, Al Harahap, Jerry Won Lee, and Ana Ribero.

My colleagues in the Department of Writing and Rhetoric Studies at the University of Utah gave me my big break in 2017. The early stages of writing this book happened in their dwelling. Jenny Andrus, Nona Brown, Jay Jordan, Maureen Mathison, Joy Pierce, Natalie Stillman-Webb, Jon Stone, and Christie Toth all made me believe I was a part of their crew. Outside the department at the University of Utah, Kent Ono continues to be especially supportive as a mentor. Annie Fukushima got me plugged in. Special thanks go to Kathryn Bond Stockton, for making it possible to meet and work with my brother, Romeo García. Romeo and I were hired together at Utah, where we bonded over a shared commitment to theory and fought about the stakes of Latinamericanist decolonial thought. We've spent thousands of hours eating, thinking, and writing together since the day we met. This book is better because of him.

The University of Oregon is my research home. I thank Gabe Paquette for granting me an extension to my tenure clock due to COVID-19-related disruptions to my research. Thank you also to Patrick Phillips, Bruce Blonigen, Harry Wonham, and Mark Whalan for supporting my extension. Additionally, I would like to thank the incredible team at the Oregon Humanities Center—Paul Peppis, Jena Turner, Melissa Gustafson, Peg Freas Gearhart—for the subvention grant the OHC provided to support the publication of this book. I express deep gratitude and respect to my department chair, Mark Whalan, who has had my back since the day I arrived on campus. Sarah Wald's unwavering support gave me courage when I ran out of it. She has fed me, picked morels out of the ashes of wildfires with me, and shown me how to find joy in every blade of grass. I am forever grateful to my colleagues in Latinx Studies who have made a home for me at the University of Oregon: Sergio Loza, Audrey Lucero, Ernesto Martínez, Gabriela Martínez, Adriana Miramontes Olivas, Yvette Saavedra, Lynn Stephen, and Ed Wolfe. Avinnash Tiwari took me to his garden many times and taught me how to cultivate brotherly love. Chiara Gasparini has loved me for who I am and spent many hours eating fried air with me. I would like to thank the following University of Oregon colleagues and staff members who have supported me along the way: Faith Barter, Melissa Bowers, Kirby Brown, Mattie Burkert, Mike Copperman, Ashley Cordes, Jim Crosswhite, Maria Fernanda Escallón, Tara Fickle, David Frank, John Gage, Sangita Gopal, Michael Hames García, Julie Heffernan, Anne Laskaya, Christina Lujin, Michelle McKinley, Quinn Miller, Nicolae Morar, Shannon Mockli, Susan Myers, Tia North, Brendan O'Kelly, Chris Paulson, Siobhan Rockcastle, Camisha Russell, Emily Simnitt, Tze-Yin Teo, and David Yorgesen. Additionally, I have also been lucky to work with wonderful graduate students: Travis Heeren, Teresa Hernández, Audrey Kalman, June Manuel, and Madhura Nadarajah. Their influence is marked throughout this book.

My colleagues in rhetorical studies have given so much of their time to help me write this book. Thank you to the following people who have shown up to my talks, presented with me, and provided feedback to my ideas in a variety of venues: Kristin Arola, Adam Banks, Casey Boyle, Gabe Carter, Christina

Cedillo, Diane Davis, Eric House, Brad Jacobson, Michael Kennedy, LuMing Mao, Cruz Medina, Jaime Armin Mejílla, Casie Moreland, Ersula Ore, Amanda Pratt, Thomas Rickert, Abraham Romney, Raúl Sánchez, Nathan Stormer, Karrieann Soto Vega, Victor Vitanza, and Hua Zhu.

In Oregon, I have a community of people who have surrounded me with unconditional support. Thank you to Ryan Adams, Romain Bauer, Dan Bentley, Doug and Shaunae Caverly, Caleb Connolly, Matt Demianew, Rob Eller, Lindsey Foltz, Sean Fontenot, Leah Pitcher, Jesse Wendel, and Carolyn Williams.

I offer my indebtedness to my family. My parents, Dawn and José, have loved me unconditionally and made it possible for me to live a life of the mind. My sister, Amanda, and her partner, Paul, have been patient listening to me ramble over many hours. They also don't let me take myself too seriously and have been wonderful elders to my children. Speaking of children, both of mine were born during the writing of this book. Finn and Reyna are two of the most fearless thinkers I know. Neither of them is afraid to ask questions: *Why don't you have hair on your head? Who made the Earth? Where do babies come from? Where did Grandpa go when he died? Why do I have to go to school today?* Their relentless questioning is equal parts inspiring and challenging, 'cause I don't have all the answers. But they aren't afraid to ask questions, and I love wandering in thought with them. If they ever read these pages, I hope they'll have remembered how curious they were at seven and four, and I hope they will have known just how much their fearlessness helped me to remember mine.

My partner, Dana, has been my biggest supporter for going on fourteen years now. She took Finn and Reyna to Long Beach, Colville, Enchanted Forest, Portland, and many other places for many nights by herself so I could finish this book. She is our mountain in the central Oregon Cascades. How lucky our family is to live and grow in her rain shadow, where we have found the most abundant and enjoyable rainfall.

Sections of chapter 2 originally appeared in *Philosophy and Rhetoric* 51, no. 2 (2018), https://doi.org/10.5325/philrhet.51.2.0124. An earlier version of chapter 3 was published previously in *Journal for the History of Rhetoric* 24, no. 1 (2021), https://doi.org/10.1080/26878003.2021.1881312. A section of chapter 4 originally appeared in *Philosophy and Rhetoric* 55, no. 1 (2022), https://doi.org/10.5325/philrhet.55.1.0097. An earlier version of chapter 5 was published previously in *Rhetorics of Democracy in the Americas*, edited by Adriana Angel, Michael L. Butterworth, and Nancy R. Gómez (University Park: Pennsylvania State University Press, 2021). They are reprinted with permission from Pennsylvania State University Press.

Introduction | "A Pesar de Todo"

> A political agenda informed by and accounting for the sheer heterogeneity of *los que
> nunca llegarán* obtains now as the only challenge available that critically engages the
> conditions defining the contemporary at the U.S.-Mexico border.
> —Abraham Acosta, *Thresholds of Illiteracy: Theory, Latin America,
> and the Crisis of Resistance*

The Mural of Hope for Migrants, painted by Ivan Herrera in Nogales, Mexico,
stands across the street from the Nogales-Morley Gate Port of Entry, where
thousands of people cross the U.S.-Mexico border on foot each day (fig. 1).[1] The
Spanish text on the mural reads, "HERE IN THE NORTH YOUR NAME LIVES ON
DESPITE EVERYTHING," in capital letters, as if shouted in the form of a demand.
The mural, Herrera explains, was dedicated to undocumented migrants who
lost their lives in the desert attempting to cross into the United States. *Acá* can
be translated to "here" in English. But opposed to *aquí*, which signifies a more
defined location that is in close proximity, *acá* signifies a general, less defined
"here." *Acá* can also signify "here," as in "where I am, but you aren't." Where is
"ACÁ EN EL NORTE," then? *El Norte* is slang for "the United States"; however, the
"acá" in the mural doesn't signify a definite location. For one thing, the mural is
located in Nogales, Sonora, Mexico, not Nogales, Arizona, U.S.A. And even as
the needle on the compass is oriented toward the north (the mural is painted on
a southeast-facing wall), it's unclear, in the context of "ACÁ" whether "el norte"
refers to the cardinal direction, the United States, or a kind of annex of the
United States in Sonora. Furthermore, to whom is the mural addressed? There
is an address to "los que nunca llegarán," in Abraham Acosta's words, to "those
who will never arrive" in El Norte—either at a destination in the United States
after a journey or in attaining political intelligibility as someone worthy of love

Fig. 1 | Ivan Herrera, *El Mural de la Esperanza para los Migrantes* (The mural of hope for migrants). Nogales, Sonora, Mexico, 31°1957.3 N, 110°5632.1 W. Photograph by author.

and hospitality.[2] If the mural addresses lost undocumented migrants, those who would be the referent of "тú," then its intended recipient will have never received its message.

The mural communicates an inexpressible truth, one lacking a place and language to communicate it in the postnational context of the U.S.-Mexico borderlands.[3] In addressing those who will have never received its message, the mural affirms the existence of those who experience what Lisa Cacho might call "social death."[4] In the United States, undocumented migrants are located in a political impasse: empirically, undocumented migrants are *here*, taking part in the economy by producing gross domestic product (GDP) through labor productivity, for example. Politicians acknowledge as much when they incorrectly suggest that undocumented immigrants "take our jobs." Rhetorically, however, undocumented migrants are *not here*, having not yet arrived into intelligibility as political subjects, according to the law and public arguments.[5]

Despite this, however, the mural issues a nonhermeneutic rhetoric that is exorbitant and out of place (atopic) in the order of the postnational U.S.-Mexico borderlands, disrupting the "symbolic distribution of bodies" by addressing those who had no business being addressed.[6] To draw in metalepsis from Diane Davis, what is communicated in the mural is not "semantic meaning but communicability as such: both a shared exposedness, a 'we' that precedes and exceeds hermeneutic understanding, and an attendant rhetorical imperative, a responsibility to respond."[7] The mural communicates irrationally, for that is the language available to address the atopic subject position of *los que nunca llegarán*. Or perhaps, as Michelle Ballif argues, "regarding the dead, guarding them, mourning them, is the ethical relation that makes any rhetorical address possible."[8] Such an address is not simply an act of public memory; it exposes us to a rhetorical imperative: to see those whom we've learned to not see (for seeing is not simply a biological process but also a rhetorical one) and to see this ongoing crisis of lost migrants as itself irrational and unacceptable.

The Mural of Hope for Migrants addresses an ongoing crisis of human rights at the U.S.-Mexico border. Since 1994, the U.S. Border Patrol has intentionally militarized urban ports of entry along the U.S.-Mexico border to persuade undocumented migrants to attempt crossing into the U.S. through inhospitable rural terrain like the Sonoran Desert in southern Arizona. Border Patrol calls this strategy "Prevention Through Deterrence." Border Patrol wagers that closing urban crossing routes will reroute undocumented migrants to instead seek entry in punishing desert terrain that itself might prevent "illegal" immigration. And depending on how you look at it, Border Patrol has found success with deterrence. According to Border Patrol figures, 1.01 people have died or disappeared per day attempting to enter the U.S. through the U.S.-Mexico border between 1998 and 2019.[9] However, a coauthored report issued by No Más Muertes (a ministry of the Unitarian Universalist Church of Tucson) and La Coalición de Derechos Humanos (a Tucson-based grassroots organization) suggests, "While Border Patrol itself claims an official count of 7,805 remains recovered from 1998 through 2019, our team estimates that three to ten times as many people may have died or disappeared since the implementation of Prevention through Deterrence."[10] And the problem appears to be intensifying. In 2022, for example, 686 migrants died or disappeared on the U.S.-Mexico border, a rate of 1.88 per day, "making it the deadliest land route for migrants worldwide on record."[11] To prevent illegal entry by deterrence at the U.S.-Mexico border, the United States has been making undocumented migrants disappear.

Luis Alberto Urrea's landmark book *The Devil's Highway: A True Story* documents the fallout of Prevention Through Deterrence by investigating the story of the Wellton 26, a group of twenty-six undocumented migrants from Mexico who walked into the United States in western Pima County, Arizona, in May 2001. The migrants were from Veracruz, where the North American Free Trade Agreement (NAFTA), which also went into effect in

1994, was undermining local economies. Unable to feed their families, the migrants turned to human traffickers, who charged them exorbitant prices to traffic them across the U.S.-Mexico border and, eventually, abandon them in the Sonoran Desert in Arizona. Of the twenty-six who entered Arizona, twelve survived and fourteen died from exposure to the extreme conditions of the desert.

Published in 2004, *The Devil's Highway* became a reservoir of rhetorical energy for public arguments about U.S. immigration policy under Prevention Through Deterrence, nearly winning a Pulitzer Prize in 2005 in the General Nonfiction category.[12] In its nonfiction form, *The Devil's Highway* sets out to excavate the details of the migrants' journey and the wider sociopolitical conditions under which such an event could have occurred. One of the defining qualities of the text is a rhetorical impasse in its structure: *The Devil's Highway* narrates the urgency to know and disclose the event of undocumented migrant deaths and the simultaneous impossibility of such a task. Urrea documents the history of the Wellton 26 from witness testimony from Border Patrol agents and surviving migrants, forensic evidence from the Pima County Office of the Medical Examiner, and Border Patrol documents and video recordings. Additionally, in moments when the archaeological truth of the migrants' journey is foreclosed by a lack of information regarding how and where the migrants and their coyotes became lost in the Arizona desert, Urrea turns to invention: "As they walked they started to lose themselves. Their accounts of the following days fade into a strange twilight of pain. Names are forgotten. Locations are nebulous, at best, since none of them, not even the Coyotes, even knew where they were. Nameless mountains loomed over them, nameless stars burned mutely overhead, nameless demons gibbered from the nameless canyons."[13] Urrea supplements the absence of reliable information with a rhetorical invention that is at once both an addition and a substitution to the history of the Wellton 26.

Before I proceed, I want to frame my reading with a caveat. Adolfo Béjar Lara fairly criticizes *The Devil's Highway* for narrativizing undocumented migrants under an ethics of economic injustice, in case readers become complacent in seeing undocumented migration as appropriate only when subjects are looking for work. Béjar Lara writes, "In 'delivering' the Wellton 26 as a group of men looking for improved economic opportunities amid neoliberal devastation, *The Devil's Highway* reproduces a social imaginary that continues to narrativize migration as an effect of neoliberal economic governance and not as a key feature of how neoliberalism reproduces and consolidates itself through dispossession and exploitation."[14] This is an important point. According to Béjar Lara, conversations about undocumented migration from Latin America can focus on the production of undocumented migrant subjectivities under the heading of primitive accumulation, for, "in a historical moment where authoritarianism is fueling xenophobia, it is necessary to reject the 'delivery systems' that make migrants legible as subjects of economic injustice and human rights, and it becomes urgent to center migrants as agents of a hemispheric struggle against the neoliberal violence causing the forcible displacement of thousands of communities in Mexico and Central America."[15]

At any rate, I don't mean to suggest here that there's a deficit in Urrea's writing or that his invention contaminated the truth of what really happened to the Wellton 26. I suggest precisely the opposite: perhaps *The Devil's Highway* is a true story of an abundant semiotic exorbitance structuring the narrative, incapable of complete documentation. In fact, a complete history of their journey—the deaths of the fourteen members of the Wellton 26, their recruitment into a transnational network of human trafficking, and perhaps even whom to hold accountable for their deaths—will remain obscured. In another example, reviewing sheriff's department footage of the twelve survivors after they were rescued, Urrea writes, "They're in shock. They can't spell their own names. They can't spell the names of the villages and ranches they came from. They look to the deputies, as if the Americans can help them remember the letters. They don't know what day it is. They don't know the name of where they were. When they mention Sonoita, they call it 'Sonorita,' or Little Sonora. 'Do you know which direction you traveled?' the sheriff asks one man. He thinks for a moment, then nods. 'Yes, I remember,' he says. He gestures straight ahead with one hand. 'That way,' he says."[16] It's not that this survivor's one-handed gesture is semiotically meaningless because it doesn't match the actual direction they traveled, for the survivor's invention here discloses a different kind of truth than the one *The Devil's Highway* set out to excavate: this is a true story of a rhetoricity that dominant historical discourse could never completely appropriate.

In this book, I examine rhetorics of undocumented migration in the Prevention Through Deterrence era that unsettle the idea of documentation as a tool for producing knowledge about politics in the U.S.-Mexico borderlands. I study modes of rhetorical invention in public arguments about immigration that take shape in what I'm provisionally calling rhetorical disinvention: fissures of emergent and exorbitant rhetoricity immanent in every act of documentation that escape apprehension but nevertheless produce politics. I study how state officials draw from commonplaces of documentation and securitization to form persuasive strategies to justify deterrence tactics of immigration enforcement. I also study how writers, artists, activists, and nongovernmental organizations (NGOs) draw from the same commonplaces to develop persuasive strategies for challenging deterrence tactics of immigration enforcement. As I juxtapose these rhetorical practices, I observe unintended and semiotic anomalies emerging within mutually exclusive appeals to documentation that produce unintended political effects and expose readers to a form of truth that Michel Foucault, reading Friedrich Nietzsche, calls an "error, insofar as it is violence done to knowledge," unable to be put to work in the name of any hegemony.[17]

I take a transdisciplinary rhetorical approach—combining rhetorical analysis, discourse analysis, historiography, and poststructuralism—to evaluate Prevention Through Deterrence–era rhetorics of undocumented migration at the U.S.-Mexico border and the conceptual language I have inherited for doing this work. I pull together scholarship on the U.S.-Mexico border from rhetorical studies, Latin American cultural studies, and Latinx cultural studies. One reason for this approach is that it is difficult to define the ontological and disciplinary scope of national boundaries. Even as scholars can arrive at nominalist ideas about the U.S.-Mexico borderlands as a site of political space, rhetorical invention, and literary imagination, these topoi and tropes always seem to migrate beyond their conceptual boundaries. How far does any borderlands extend in each direction, anyway? Should the U.S.-Mexico border fall under the domain of Latin American studies or Latinx studies? Neither or both? I make no attempt to resolve that tension in this book, and I seek out a confluence of "disciplinary exposure," in Erin Graff Zivin's terms, to unsettle the expropriation of the U.S.-Mexico border as a site of inquiry under the dominion of any discipline. This exposure, Graff Zivin suggests, might yet "reveal the defective quality of the sovereignty or autonomy of each, the 'points of untranslatability' that simultaneously constitute and unsettle disciplinary thinking."[18]

Before I provide an overview of *Disinventions* in this introductory chapter, I need to unpack the title and load-bearing concepts that I've just presented. But first, a few words on my own locus of enunciation.

I am employed by a settler-colonial public institution of higher education in the United States. You'd be right to question how I, a scholar employed to produce knowledge under and through an ideological state apparatus, could propose to study what I just described as a discursive form that couldn't be appropriated by the very nation-state I answer to. In writing this book, wouldn't committing to the archive a study of subalternity in the U.S.-Mexico borderlands amount to an appropriation? Would I not be hand-delivering knowledge about subalternized peoples to the nation-state and, in turn, making it easier for that state to hegemonize? Would I not be, in Ranajit Guha's words, writing the "prose of counter-insurgency"?[19] My answer will likely not be satisfying, but here it is anyway: this book is my effort to throw a wrench into the gears of power/knowledge. I won't claim to be able to read something that the nation-state cannot read, and I won't claim that I have the secret to unlocking a nonnormative form of decolonial political resistance. Instead, I write about sites of unintelligibility immanent to hegemony that interrupt its processes of signification from an atopic position that Gayatri Spivak defined as subalternity, or "the absolute limit of the place where history is narrativized into logic."[20] I make descriptive statements on the disruptive effects these sites of unintelligibility produce, which, I wager, describe hegemony's finitude and politics' openings. I postulate that even in a world defined by what Antonio Negri calls the "total subsumption of society" under capital, there remains a practice of critical thought that could disrupt the terrain of knowledge production in which it is grounded.[21] Negri suggests that after 1968, capitalist production has outgrown industrial production and become diffuse in subsuming even the most local forms of social production. The implication here is that there is no longer an outside to capitalism's modes of organization and representation, to the degree that such a location beyond global capitalism's modes of representation would be already constitutive of it. There's no location beyond capital from which to read it. Despite this, I postulate that one can still engage a permanent labor of the negative that can desediment the terrain of knowledge production from which it is grounded and join in a collective effort to confront what Slavoj Žižek calls the "constitutive lie of University Discourse," which "disavows its performative dimension, presenting what effectively amounts to a political decision based on power as a simple insight into the factual state of things."[22] My reading of disinvention serves as a reminder to "fight the tendential reduction of thinking to the condition of a means for the technical reproduction of what there is."[23] Instead of trying to apprehend undocumented immigration—to more efficiently know, capture, and fear others—I attempt to make what Jacques

Derrida calls a "passive decision" to observe incalculable places and identities in the U.S.-Mexico borderlands and ask after the responsibilities of addressing those who have yet to arrive.[24]

Disinvention as Concept

In this book, I use the term "disinvention" in an antanaclastic doubled sense: as (1) an emergent and exorbitant rhetoricity that escapes apprehension but is nevertheless productive of politics;[25] and (2) a mode of rhetorical analysis for reading undocumented migration in "error, insofar as it is violence done to knowledge," beyond the will to apprehend.[26]

By "disinvention," I don't refer to a minoritarian subject's strategies of rhetorical invention or cultural production to resist dominant discourses. Instead, I refer to disinvention as an emergent property, irreducible to individual subjects.[27] I build on and depart from José Esteban Muñoz's theory of disidentification. Whereas I depart from his idea of disidentification as "strategies that are called on by minoritarian subjects," I look to generalize Muñoz's reading of an emergent property of Felix Gonzalez-Torres's art that "potentially informs an *anti-identitarian identity politics* in which commonality is not forged through shared images and fixed identifications but fashioned instead from connotative images that invoke communal structures of feelings."[28] Additionally, my use of the term is informed by Spivak's description of rhetoric *not* as a system of tropology but as an emergent property of semiosis—as "the name for the residue of indeterminacy which escapes the system" and "what escapes even an exhaustive system of tropological analysis."[29] Disinvention does not name a process by which a minoritarian subject produces identification or persuasion. Instead, it is the name for an emergent rhetoricity that can't be apprehended but nevertheless produces politics. By "politics," I refer to Jacques Rancière's definition, which signifies an interruption in the rhetorical process of civic administration:

> Political activity is whatever shifts a body from the place assigned to it or changes a place's destination. It makes visible what had no business being seen, and makes heard a discourse where once there was only place for noise; it makes understood as discourse what was once only heard as noise. . . . Political activity is always a mode of expression that undoes the perceptible divisions of the police order by implementing a basically

heterogeneous assumption, that of a part of those who have no part, an assumption that, at the end of the day, itself demonstrates the sheer contingency of the order, the equality of any speaking being with any other speaking being.[30]

As the name for an interruption in a grid of civic knowledge, politics does not yield a calculus for civic administration. Rancière defines politics as a kind of solvent to what he calls "police": "Politics is generally seen as the set of procedures whereby the aggregation and consent of collectivities is achieved, the organization of powers, the distribution of places and roles, and the systems for legitimizing this distribution. I propose to give this system of distribution and legitimization another name. I propose to call it *the police*."[31] Policing, in addition to the paramilitary branch of material legal force in the United States, is a rhetorical force circulating through commonplaces, "an order of bodies that defines the allocation of ways of doing, ways of being, and ways of saying, and sees that those bodies are assigned by name to a particular place and task; it is an order of the visible and the sayable that sees that a particular activity is visible and another is not, that this speech is understood as discourse and another as noise."[32]

Speaking of commonplaces, this book sheds new light on topical theories of rhetoric by examining disinvention as an emergent rhetoricity issued from without commonplace.[33] According to Christa Olson, "the commonplace is the basic terrain of rhetoric," and "topoi [are] nodes of social value and common sense that provide places of return for convening arguments across changing circumstances."[34] Ralph Cintrón defines topoi as "storehouses of energy" that "organize our sentiments, beliefs, and actions in the lifeworld."[35] Olson and Cintrón suggest that topoi provide rhetoric with force. Commonplaces are, in Rancière's words, the discursive infrastructure for enforcing "ways of doing, ways of being, and ways of saying." How, then, to conceptualize rhetoric issued from without commonplace?

My proposition is that disinvention is the name for an atopic weak force issued from without commonplace, or from without antecedent shared meaning. In recent years, scholars of rhetoric have developed the concept of atopos to name phenomena that don't quite fit the criteria of topos.[36] Michele Kennerly writes, "Literally, atopos means 'without a place,' or 'out of place.' . . . The underlying semantic unity is that whoever or whatever deemed to warrant the adjective *atopos* have dared disturb someone's sense of order of things, such that sorting things out has become necessary once again."[37] Atopos designates a sub-ject position that is "out of place" in society and that cannot be narrativized into any dominant logic. Foucault refers to this condition as "loss of what is 'common' to place and name. Atopia."[38]

By "weak force," I refer to a rhetoricity issued from beyond apprehension. I have in mind what Jacques Derrida identified as an incalculable and noncoercive weak force of influence, a "force without power [that] opens up unconditionally to what or who comes and comes to affect it."[39] This weak force would not force shared meaning or common experience and would not influence from mutual intelligibility. In this sense, disinvention would be incompatible with the force of topos: "No politics, no ethics, and no law can be, as it were, deduced from this thought. To be sure, nothing can be done [*faire*] with it."[40]

Disinvention as Method

I also use the term "disinvention" to refer to a mode of rhetorical analysis for read-ing undocumented migration in "error, insofar as it is violence done to knowledge," beyond the will to apprehend.[41] In the case studies that follow this introduction, I read apprehension as a commonplace of power/knowledge. Apprehension is a topos of securitization in U.S. federal immigration discourse with a semantic range that includes "to understand," "to capture," and "to fear an unpleasant future event." But apprehension also appears as a topos in public arguments that seek to render understandings of undocumented migration toward the ends of forming a less harmful form of immigration policy. Following cues from Karma Chávez's and María Josefina Saldaña-Portillo's critiques of citizenship as a commonplace of policing, in *Disinventions* I depart from locating undocumented migration as a site of practical reasoning for immigration policy reform.[42]

I argue that a better understanding of the crises wrought by Prevention Through Deterrence isn't available, for there are no topoi from which to invent the right words to be issued at the opportune time, by the right speaker, to persuade those who are unwilling to extend hospitality to undocumented migrants. The use of topoi *to force* a change of mind in someone else would be to wield rhetoric as a force to justify an injustice, for who am I to force someone to change their mind anyway? After all, rhetoric is not alchemy or incantation. Metaethical questions aside, there is no reason to believe that a better under-standing (in, for example, the possession of more or complete data sets) of the consequences of Prevention Through Deterrence would serve to humanize migrants to the nation-state and lead to the abolition of oppressive immigration enforcement practices. Even the cruelest photographs of undocumented migrants, for example, have yet to do so. And yet, like *The Mural of Hope for Migrants*, a disinvention issued from within such photographs exposes us to an infrapolitical demand that is "out of place" in the current regime of settler-colonialism—to a demand for what Derrida names as an "*unconditional hospitality* that exposes itself without limit to the coming of the other, beyond rights and laws, beyond a hospitality conditioned by the right of asylum, by the right to immigration, by citizenship, and even by the right to universal hospitality."[43] By "infrapolitical," I defer to the political scientist and anthropologist James Scott, for whom infrapolitics designates acts, techniques, signs, and thoughts that are not yet perceived as politics, or, exceptions to the rule of political perception.[44] Rhetorical studies has been here before, specifically, with questions about the nature of rhetorical invention. For example, is the infrapolitical, then, that grounding which comes before politics, which Geoffrey Bennington has suggested is the domain of rhetoric?[45] Or is infrapolitics *politics par excellence*, a domain of truth beyond grandstanding and bullshitting that "punches a hole in knowledge"?[46]

Why This Book?

So why a rhetorical book on rhetorics of undocumented migration in the Prevention Through Deterrence era? Proceeding from Alberto Moreiras's claim that "university discourse today can move along the lines of a reduction of the world to a principle of accounting, following the neoliberal subjection of the real to representational calculation; or it can proceed along the lines of a reduction of the world to a principle of accountability," in *Disinventions* I reflect on the limits of producing positive knowledge about undocumented migration under the will to apprehend.[47] I am not interested in brandishing technologies of documentation to account for the archaeological truth about undocumented migrants in the U.S.-Mexico borderlands. In any case, as the anthropologist Jason De León argues in his landmark study of Prevention Through Deterrence, "No matter what you do, you can never get full comprehension of what is actually happening on our southern frontier. The system in place has too many moving parts traveling at sometimes blinding speed. Your view of any single part is blurry at best. But it doesn't matter what you can actually see, because there are always things going on out of sight."[48]

This book is not a cultural history of the U.S.-Mexico borderlands. It is also not about how authors and speakers have drawn from borderlands commonplaces to construct arguments or enact new modes of political thought. Scholars of border rhetorics and Latinx studies have already documented this phenomenon well.[49] I think alongside border rhetoricians to read the border not simply as a physical zone that lends itself as a referent to discursive practice but also as exception to place and name altogether. Even as the physical manifestation of national boundary divisions sometimes appears *as place* (for example, on U.S.-American territory, north of the Rio Grande at the McAllen-Hidalgo crossing in Texas), the U.S.-Mexico border line itself marks an exception *to place* altogether. Area calculations for a national territory, for example, do not include the border line; the border itself lacks discrete coordinates and is only implied in calculations as a plane's edge. The border itself stands neither in the United States nor in Mexico but instead draws both territories into relief *as places*. The rhetoricity of the border, in its discrete placelessness, produces difference, and border rhetorics scholars have critiqued how this difference informs racial and xenophobic underpinnings of policies, legislation, and other public rhetorics to highlight their lasting implications on public rhetorics, subject formation, and policy in the United States.[50] Indeed, as Lisa Flores has shown, the violence and suffering of migrants are rooted not in a lack of information about the situation but in white supremacist imaginaries and mundane disregard.[51] Others have investigated the border as both a site and effect of rhetorical invention and, in turn, have sought to examine how individuals and groups have wielded the rhetoricities of the border to advance claims on political belonging. D. Robert DeChaine argues, for example, that "a rhetorical border studies offers the potential for a counterhegemonic intervention."[52] I want to add a new layer to border rhetorics scholarship that builds on, and takes off from, the important rhetorical work of scholars like Karma Chávez, J. David Cisneros, Lisa Flores, and Ana Milena Ribero by adding to the conversation readings of rhetorical disinvention that escape their violent framing and outline a possibility for thought beyond even counterhegemonic apprehensions. I share with these scholars a common goal, which is not simply to reintroduce the spectacle of suffering under an exciting new grammar but the abolition of policies that by design produce violent spectacles of migrant suffering as pretexts for oppressive immigration policies. Instead of framing this project within a genealogy of counterhegemonic politics, I situate it, following the work of Abraham Acosta, Erin Graff Zivin, Andrés Guzmán, Alberto Moreiras, and Gareth Williams, within a genealogy of ideas about posthegemony, a term that I define in more detail in chapter 4.

I also need to take a few words to situate this book methodologically in an ongoing Latinx and Latinamericanist discussion about the politics of knowledge production. Given the important decolonial scholarship across the borders of Latin American studies and Latinx studies that I have inherited, I need to explain why *Disinventions* is not an outright decolonial book. *Disinventions* retreats from the methodological premise that a study of people in Latin America or in the United States from Latin American diaspora should reject European ideas in favor of ideas that are homegrown, so to speak. I am not suggesting that every scholar holds this assumption—or even that scholarship proceeding from this assumption is homogeneous or unimportant. I suggest instead that the act of inheritance (of receiving property, knowledges, and cultural practices that one did not actively choose) is a bit more complicated than rejecting the unsavory parts of an inheritance for the savory bits. As a Latinx person examining rhetorical production by and about Latinx and Latin American diasporic people, I have inherited a mass of critical thought with a complicated history. I don't have the space to detangle that history of ideas in this book. I will, however, position myself in a complicated inheritance of theories of decoloniality and explain why I think through a genealogy of deconstruction that cites ideas from writers on both sides of the Atlantic.

At any rate, it is now commonplace in Latinx and Latin American cultural studies to suggest that critical ideas that originate from Europe, including theories of hegemony, are insufficient to account for the histories of modernization and power in the Americas. Latinamericanist varieties of decolonial thought emerge from a genealogy of scholarship including scholars like Aníbal Quijano, Walter Mignolo, and Enrique Dussel. Dussel argues, for example, that

> modernity is, in fact, a European phenomenon, but one constituted in a dialectical relation with a non-European alterity that is its ultimate content. Modernity appears when Europe affirms itself as the "center" of a World History that it inaugurates; the "periphery" that surrounds this center is consequently part of its self-definition. The occlusion of this periphery (and of the role of Spain and Portugal in the formation of the modern world system from the late fifteenth to the mid-seventeenth centuries) leads the major contemporary thinkers of the "center" into a

Eurocentric fallacy in their understanding of modernity. If their understanding of the genealogy of modernity is thus partial and provincial, their attempts at a critique or defense of it are likewise unilateral and, in part, false.[53]

Dussel's influential reading of Western modernity describes the rhetorical conditions constitutive of a type of power/knowledge that came to be known as "Eurocentricity": a rhetorical process whereby the telling of history and politics of others from a unilateral point of view becomes a pretext justifying the colonization of the Americas. Western modernity is *invented* in a topos that is its constitutive condition of possibility, or its "non-European alterity that is its ultimate content." Western modernity is a rhetorical invention that appears in a dialectical relation *with*, not before or after, its opposite. Still, for Dussel, a critique of Eurocentricity must come from a place outside Europe.

In recent years, rhetorical studies of Latin America and the U.S.-Mexico borderlands have become structured by an analytical presupposition about truth inherited from an injunction to disclose and know alterity that shaped a particular branch of Latinamericanist thought in the 1990s. As Graff Zivin writes about this branch of Latinamericanism, "This excavational mode of thought, a cousin of a certain conservative philological tendency, has as its foundation or ground—in addition to what is built upon it—that which hides beneath it, an identifiable and revealable truth."[54] Critics have come to assume that there is a repressed truth located within rhetorical, literary, and cultural forms that, when discovered, will provide the source material for a politics of emancipation from Eurocentricity. A good deal of rhetorical and cultural criticism has become fundamentally structured by this will to know and disclose alterity.

It is also now commonplace to argue that the originary event of colonialism— the violent expropriation of Indigenous land, culture, and bodies by European groups in the fifteenth century and the process of cultural and racial miscegenation that unfolded from it—produces a subject position that is inherently resistant to what Walter Mignolo, for example, has identified as the matrix of modernity/coloniality. This subject is often genealogically grounded in the discourse of mestizaje, understood by critics as an exceptional form of Latin American hybridity. The mestiza serves as the figure of this mixture between incommensurate ethnoracial groups and the source material for a politics of decolonization. And in contemporary rhetorical criticism, the U.S.-Mexico borderlands has come to assume the qualities of mestizaje and, in turn, serve as a topos, a ground zero, for this decolonial turn. The consequence of this reading for Latin American rhetorical and cultural criticism is an overemphasis on theories and reading practices assuming, as Charles Hatfield describes, "that cultural practices can be logically justified on the grounds that they are ours" and that the "celebration of cultural difference is a form of resistance to neoliberalism."[55] This critical mode takes the shape of what Moreiras has identified as Latinamericanism's constitutive double injunction: the injunction to both reduce and preserve difference as its constitutive object of study.[56] As I have argued with Romeo García, what we are witnessing across rhetorical studies, too, is a genuine attempt to theorize an alternative form of subjectivity in order to revitalize a praxis of difference.[57]

In Latinamericanist circles, decoloniality emerges out of the conversations of subalternity in the 1980s. In chapter 2, I argue that decoloniality, as a modality of thought that emerges from Walter Mignolo's readings of Enrique Dussel and Aníbal Quijano, reaches a methodological impasse from its readings of subalternity as a nonideological practice of reading. In other words, with these accounts of subalternity as the kernel of a non-Western, nonideological exteriority, we get an irreducibly doubled enunciation of subaltern semiosis as *both* language itself and the ideological accounting of that language. If the problem is ideology itself—a metalepsis in the act of taking account of the subaltern subject-effect through the language of Western coloniality—then there is simply no way of scrubbing ideology without also evacuating language itself because we get both at the same time. We simply cannot do away with ideology in the practice of reading. I don't necessarily believe that this impasse is a bad thing, however. I believe that there is opportunity to take it up as a site of invention. Homi Bhabha argues that it is an ambivalence that makes the political possible in the first place, for political positions are "always a process of translation and transference of meaning . . . constructed on the trace of that perspective that it puts under erasure."[58]

There is unfinished business with ideas about subalternity that are implied in theories of decoloniality. Recall the first sentences of Gayatri Chakravorty Spivak's essay "Can the Subaltern Speak?": "Some of the most radical criticism coming out of the West today is the result of an interested desire to conserve the subject of the West, or the West as Subject. The theory of pluralized 'subject effects' gives an illusion of undermining subjective sovereignty while often providing a cover for this subject of knowledge." Over the rest of the essay,

Spivak analyzes the rhetorical function of poststructuralism and argues that the "critique of the sovereign subject thus actually inaugurates a subject." There is a constitutive function of representation that seems to get lost in the persistent intellectual injunction to "disclose and know the discourse of society's Other."[59] It is as if these sites of alterity themselves signify something beyond the capacity of the reader, as if they possess a capacity for rhetorical invention that has yet to receive its due. I wager that the unfinished business of subalternity, which remains impassive more than thirty years after the publication of Spivak's essay, can yield yet more insight both about the rhetorical cultures of immigration enforcement at the U.S.-Mexico borderlands *and* about the critical resources that I have inherited for reading these cultures.

Critics have often grounded their readings in the stakes of Spivak's landmark essay. The prevailing response to Spivak's question has been to develop an interpretive strategy *outside* the terms and conditions of Western imperialism, grounded in an authentic (non-Western) subaltern subject position, to scrub ideology from representation so that alterity might finally have its say. The debates turn on a postulation of the identity of subalternity as "radically resistant political expressions" beyond Western influence, which Acosta argues "emerges as a result of a tacit conflation of certain ontological and logocentric guarantees that confuses assertions of heterogeneity $(A = -(-A))$ with the promise of a positive, substantive, and differential identity with which not only to critique hegemony but to challenge for it $(A = B)$."[60] The problem, however, is that within this intellectual response, (1) the identity of alterity $(A = -(-A))$ carries forward the West $(A = B)$ as an inheritance in its irreducible relation of *other as self*; and therefore, (2) this $(A = B)$ political relation is premised upon the "efface-ment of the signifier"[61]—a process of forgetting that the search for the subaltern consciousness is a critical practice that rhetorically invents subalternity.

"Can the Subaltern Speak?," then, is not a question concerning subaltern speech or a subaltern identity, per se, but one of how subaltern consciousness is invented in the act of interpretation and made to "speak" within "a post-representationalist vocabulary [hiding] an essentialist agenda."[62] This, as opposed to answering "yes," "no," or both, is a more generative way of contending with the rhetorical conditions of subalternity. As Spivak reminds us, "subaltern con-sciousness is subject to the cathexis of the élite";[63] it is not a signified but a *signi-fier*—an irreducibly constitutive subject-effect of which "the continuist and homogenist deliberative consciousness symptomatically requires a continuous and homogeneous cause for this effect and thus posits a sovereign and determining subject. This latter is, then, the effect of an effect, and its positing a metalepsis, or the substitution of an effect for a cause."[64] This metalepsis, as reflected earlier, results from the intellectual confusing of an object of study for the concept used to describe it, resulting in the substitution of a subaltern subject-effect for a "pure form of consciousness."[65] When the proposed figure of subalternity is taken as a sovereign subject, not only does the intellectual efface their role in the production of subalternity (which is the very crux of the problem of hegemonic representation) but, more importantly, the intellectual ambivalently produces, simultaneously, both subaltern speech and the account of it.

Itinerary

This book analyzes deterrence-era dominant rhetorics of political community and subject formation at the southwestern U.S.-Mexico border without subordinating itself to their logics. In addition to the theoretical argument presented in this book, *Disinventions* engages with deterrence-era political discourse at and about the southwestern U.S.-Mexico border. The analyses are arranged as an assemblage of case studies, each of which is intended to unpack specific parts of the theoretical argument. Instead of documenting a sustained historical narrative, the case studies investigate rhetorical "intensities," where disinventions rupture through and deterritorialize established grids of political intelligibility.[66] My hope is that this arrangement undermines any reduction of U.S.-Mexico border space to a topos of propriety.

Chapter 1 examines the historical shift to Prevention Through Deterrence in U.S. immigration policy and enforcement. I examine how government documents and public arguments from immigration officials draw on commonplaces of apprehension to justify deterrence. Additionally, I notice that similar common-places of apprehension appear in public arguments rebuffing deterrence policies. However, I argue that apprehension is not a commonplace that can lead to ethical reasoning that would persuade the state and abolish deterrence policies, which I read as the mark of an impasse in knowing altogether. I investigate the possibility of a rhetoricity of undocumented migration otherwise than terms and conditions of apprehension encouraged by deterrence. To do this, I read the effects of a rhetorical disinvention in the *Mapa de Migrantes Fallecidos*, a digital archive maintained by the Pima Country Office of the Medical Examiner and Humane Borders as a part of the Arizona OpenGIS Initiative for Deceased Migrants, which maps and archives more than four thousand undocumented migrant deaths in southern Arizona. Still, if apprehension cannot serve as a commonplace to invent arguments for ethical immigration policy, then it might still be read as a democratic demand that is itself *atopic*, an unplaceable and incompatible differend with the "symbolic distribution of bodies" in the current regime of settler-colonial sovereignty in the United States.[67] Instead of trying to account better, to know this crisis better as the grounds for making a better political community, it might still be possible to misapprehend the will to know that is simultaneously the will to border enforcement.

Chapter 2 assesses the state of making knowledge about cultural difference in rhetorical studies scholarship by tracing its genealogical influences in questions of cultural difference in Latin American studies, rhetorical theory, and feminist philosophy in the late 1980s and early 1990s. I read new methodological insight on the topic of cultural difference that is commonplace across scholarship, where it is often presupposed that the location from which one speaks determines the form and content of what one can say. I argue in this chapter that this premise of topical thinking genealogically grounds a good deal of scholarship that takes the border as the commonplace of a physical (the border) and/or rhetorical (borderlands) location of hybridity constituting a metaphysics of Latino subjectivity and political resistance.[68] While I am indebted to this scholarship, one of my premises is that topical/locational premises that inform cultural hybridity, border theory, and other decolonial options are not able (and were not developed to) bring descriptive power to the subjects I study. However, instead of proposing to work beyond these concepts in disavowal, I work through these concepts and their impassive qualities as part of an effort to investigate, following DeChaine, the rhetoricity of bordering and how such "bordering produces public knowledge and 'truth' about people, places, social statuses and communal allegiances."[69] I argue that it is time to consider the possibility that resisting Western epistemology from non-Western topoi (the borderlands in particular) not only is not resistant but serves as the most intimate and interior process of Eurocentrism itself. Further, if no non-Western location exists from which to critique Western hegemony, and if all that such a reading can accomplish is to provide a foundational confirmation of the latter, then perhaps we don't need to dispense with postcolonial theory more generally, but it might be time to develop new language to describe the shifts in rhetoric amid the ongoing changes to sovereignty and governmentality across the Americas.

In chapter 3, I carry forward the critical stakes raised in chapters 1 and 2 by testing the grounding of topical theorizing in the contemporary Arizona context. I begin by examining mestizocentric appeals to political inclusion from public arguments about Arizona House Bill 1070 and Arizona Senate Bill 2281, a pair of anti-immigration bills passed in 2010. I situate this reading in the context of an antecedent and ongoing form of anti-Black political exclusion going back to the colonial period in Mexico. The chapter shifts to a reading of *Las Castas*, a nineteenth-century casta painting, constitutive mestizo political philosophy that takes shape through a disinvention of Black bodies. Black and Native people weren't excluded in the system of castes—they were included as topoi of exclusion. It's therefore not simply enough to imagine a society where they are reincluded, because they were never really excluded to begin with. Rather, the problem was their toxic inclusion from the very beginning in violent, colonial rhetorics of sovereignty. In turn, chapter 3 traces the way that Black figurations of toxic inclusion escape their violent framings in their states of being "nonunderstandable" in the history of mestizaje. I draw this reading forward into the second half of the chapter to demonstrate how the arrest of a Black woman, Dr. Ersula Ore, in Arizona disinvents the mestizocentrism grounding the fight for ethnic studies in the 2010s. I argue that Dr. Ore's speech escapes the gaze of both mestizo and white onlookers on a street while she is violently arrested; what escapes in her speech is a demand that perhaps was never meant to be allowed to be issued, or a demand that was intended to be silenced by both hegemonic and counterhegemonic forces in the political battle for ethnic studies.

Chapter 3 widens the orthodox readings of the U.S.-Mexico border in rhetorical studies—which have largely focused on Mexican and Chicano communities and rhetorical practices—and asks how the grounds of rhetorical studies shift when we also address the Black subjects and bodies that have genealogically informed, and dwell in, the political space of the U.S.-Mexico border. I explore the consequences of mestizocentrism (the normative, geocultural assumption rendering the space of the U.S.-Mexico border a Mexican/Mexican American space) by reading the rhetorical production that emerged in the wake of the immigration and ethnic studies legislation in juxtaposition with Dr. Ore's arrest. As I read these case studies alongside each other, I argue that when we imagine the space of the U.S.-Mexico border via Mexican American regimes of recognition and develop a thinking of the political from these regulatory rhetorical commonplaces, not only do we prevent ourselves from coming to grips with the full complexity of the rhetorical terrain of the borderlands, but we risk reproducing the mestizocentric political legacy that has historically taken shape through the exclusion of Blackness.[70] I suggest that grounding any reading of U.S.-Mexico border space in the normative legacy of mestizocentrism effectively forecloses our ability to draw coalition among all the groups that have been and will continue to be affected by this legislation.

I conclude in chapter 1 that Prevention Through Deterrence produces a "grid of intelligibility" that frames undocumented migrants as objects of apprehension in support or opposition of immigration policy.[71] In similar fashion, I argue in chapter 4 that a better understanding of family separation is simply not available beyond its violent instrumentalization as a commonplace of arguments in disputes over federal immigration policy. In this chapter, I ask after the possibility of a rhetoricity of migrant hospitality beyond apprehension with a reflection on a photograph of Angie Valeria and Óscar Alberto Martínez Ramírez and Valeria Luiselli's testimonial *Tell Me How It Ends: An Essay in Forty Questions*. In these texts, I read a tactical misunderstanding—neither a cultivated ignorance nor an instrumentalized knowing but a will to misunderstand—of deterrence that emerges from an exorbitant rhetoricity that cannot be narrativized by power and that disinvents immigration reform as the grounds of political action. Even if representations of the trauma of family separations cannot establish commonplaces for more ethical immigration policy, I read them as a site of crisis internal to the possibility of knowing grounding a politics that Acosta describes as "a response informed by, inclusive of, and *in the non-name of All*," which "obtains now as a most critical and historical imperative: that regardless of population size or history in the area, *every* minority group has the right to assert the right to representation *anywhere*—even against the most traditional and predominant among them."[72]

In chapter 5, I continue my reading of disinvention with a historiographical account of different orders of Latinamericanism that have influenced rhetorical studies. For "Latinamericanism," I draw from Alberto Moreiras's definition: "the set or the sum total of engaged representations providing a viable knowledge of the Latin American object of enunciation." I refer to the intellectual discourse that takes Latin America as an object of study, regardless of location. I make no distinction, in other words, between Latin Americans and U.S.-Americans studying the object of Latin America. And by double injunction, I refer to the paradoxical practice of making Latin America familiar while retaining its "tropicalist" difference.[73] The chapter begins by reading Emma Perez's *The Decolonial*

Imaginary along Krista Ratcliffe's *Rhetorical Listening: Identification, Gender, Whiteness* to unpack the common theoretical assumptions about perceiving and restituting the silenced alterities on which both decolonial and rhetorical modes of historiography are premised. The chapter places this reading alongside modalities of Latinamericanist critical thought and engages directly with the second-order Latinamericanst appropriation of theories of posthegemony and infrapolitics. From there, the chapter shifts its analysis to Guillermo Gómez-Peña's *Documentado/Undocumented: Ars Shamánica Performática* and *Codex Espangliensis: From Columbus to the Border Patrol* to read an articulation of democracy at the absolute limit of the false choice between Eurocentrism and mestizaje. Whereas critics continue to theorize politics as a counterhegemonic process in which individuals circulate commonplaces of resistance as topoi of counterhegemonic cultural production from locations exterior to hegemony, I read in Gómez-Peña's work a disinvention—an errant, semiologically excessive, dimension of migrancy that operates beyond the desire to be documented as the grounding of the political. These texts suggest an infrapolitical, still-undocumented thought of politics at the limits of the capacity for knowing, producing a thought of politics as a nonnostalgic reflection on the loss of commonplace and, therefore, on politics at the absolute limits of the will to document. I then conclude the book with a postscript that discusses rhetorical theory beyond the will to apprehend.

1

Misapprehension | Prevention Through Deterrence and *Los Migrantes Fallecidos*

There is nothing radical about common sense. It would be a mistake to think that received grammar is the best vehicle for expressing radical views, given the constraints that grammar imposes upon thought, indeed, upon the thinkable itself.
—Judith Butler, *Gender Trouble: Feminism and the Subversion of Identity*

It is now commonplace knowledge that U.S.-American immigration policy and enforcement along its southwestern border is lethal.[1] In southern Arizona alone, for example, thousands of undocumented migrants have died crossing the U.S.-Mexico border. Their deaths are a consequence of "Prevention Through Deterrence," a federal southwestern border enforcement strategy developed by Sandia National Laboratories and enacted by the Immigration and Naturalization Service (INS) in 1993 that remains in effect. Today, under the deluge of xenophobia and contempt for migrants crossing the U.S.-Mexico border, migrant death is not only commonplace—it appears as self-evident and immanent to disputes over immigration policy. Public rhetorics of immigration hinge on epideictic questions accounting for blame, deliberative questions accounting for policy change, and judicial accusations accounting for violations against truth, with nearly all sides instrumentalizing topoi of undocumented migrants toward claims about the correct measure of civic administration.

Prevention Through Deterrence is the name of an immigration enforcement strategy at the U.S.-Mexico border. It is also the name for a rhetoric, a means of "making things matter," in Thomas Farrell's words, that reduces undocumented migrant bodies to objects of governmentality whose intelligibility as subjects is limited to serving as topoi of arguments in public rhetorics of immigration policy.[2] In this chapter, I investigate the possibility of a rhetoricity of undocumented migration beyond deterrence rhetorics of apprehension. U.S. Customs and Border Protection defines apprehension as "the physical control or temporary detainment of a person who is not lawfully in the U.S. which may or may not result in an arrest."[3] But apprehension has a wider semantic range that includes *to capture* and *to understand*—or, together, *to capture via understanding* and *to understand via capturing*. I argue that in the context of the deterrence era, where the will to understand migration cannot be untethered from the will to capture, apprehension offers limited potential as a critical tool for imagining a world otherwise than it is today.

I look to guide conversations beyond instrumentalizing the violent consequences of deterrence as topoi grounding a practical reasoning in the service of any form of governmentality—even benevolent reforms to federal and local immigration policy. To do this, I read the effects of a rhetorical disinvention in the *Mapa de Migrantes Fallecidos*, a digital archive maintained by the Pima Country office of the Medical Examiner and Humane Borders as a part of the Arizona OpenGIS Initiative for Deceased Migrants, which maps and archives more than four thousand undocumented migrant deaths in southern Arizona. As an archive of the missing and sometimes nameless remains of undocumented migrants, the *Mapa de Migrantes Fallecidos* is an irregular and incomplete archive, full of epistemological uncertainty that would foreclose on apprehending the true extent of the consequences of deterrence.

I read an uncapturable, exorbitant semiosis in the *Mapa de Migrantes Fallecidos* in the form of a structural misapprehension, which traces the insufficiency of apprehension as the grounds of a rhetoricity of hospitality otherwise than terms and conditions produced by deterrence. I read misapprehension as a failure to both capture and understand, as a misfired rhetorical concept for departing from the will to know and inaugurating an ethical commitment to the unforeseeable emergence of alterity.

From Obelisks to Operations

The roots of deterrence grow down to at least 1846, when the United States invaded Mexico and started the Mexican-American War. The Treaty of Guadalupe Hidalgo ended the U.S. invasion of Mexico in 1848, and the United States took 529,000 square miles of land in what is now California, Nevada, Utah, and parts of Wyoming, Colorado, Arizona, and New Mexico. Article V of the treaty defined a U.S.-Mexico international boundary along the Rio Grande in New Mexico. More "annexation" and international boundary drawing happened when the Treaty of Mesilla took effect in 1854 and the U.S. acquired 29,670 square miles of land from Mexico for $10 million. As the story goes, the treaty cut the international boundary between the two states along what is now Arizona and the western half of New Mexico.

Mary Pat Brady argues, however, that "Arizona began as a mistake." She writes, "Southern Arizona was not part of the land ceded by Mexico in the Treaty of Guadalupe Hidalgo. Instead, it was purchased in a separate agreement worked out years later. What happened? While the boundary survey commissioners were working to establish the post-1848 border near El Paso del Norte, they discovered a problem: The Disturnell Map used during treaty negotiations incorrectly located both El Paso del Norte and the Rio Bravo. The difference between the 'material' and the 'metaphorical' was not insignificant."[4] Brady suggests that Arizona was constituted in this difference between the material and the metaphorical—perhaps a result of error, perhaps a result of a less-than-honest oversight, but from a constitutive misapprehension nonetheless.

The twin cities of Nogales, Arizona, and Nogales, Sonora, began to develop in the years after this cartographic misapprehension. In 1855, only metal obelisks and rock piles marked the boundary.[5] Porfirio Díaz authorized the construction of a customs agency near the boundary in August 1880. The railroad arrived in the pass between the two communities in 1882. As Carlos Parra notes, the international community of Nogales emerged at this rhetorical difference: "Although an international boundary had always divided the two Nogales, the absence of a physical barrier stimulated the close relationship between the two cities so that, like many other border towns of the period, they were in reality one bi-national community."[6] Then, in August 1918, the U.S. government and Felix B. Peñaloza, the mayor of Nogales, Mexico, agreed to build a fence along the boundary between the two nations in Nogales in mutual good faith. Rachel St. John writes, "When [the fences] were first erected in Nogales a century ago, they were neither a brazen political statement nor a barrier to immigrants, but a cooperative measure, embraced by both the U.S. and Mexico in the spirit of 'good fences make good neighbors.'"[7] One side built one fence, the other side another, two fences standing next to each other to create a gateway through which officials could begin to document, but not apprehend, movement between the two. In Nogales, the fences weren't built to gatekeep the United States but, instead, to foster passage. The "good fences make good neighbors" ethos wouldn't last. That same month, Peñaloza was killed in the Battle of Ambos Nogales near the boundary fences.

It wasn't long before the U.S.-Mexico boundary became a topos of securitization and apprehension in U.S.-American civic imaginaries. By the late nineteenth century, the U.S. had already begun to develop a logic of deterrence with "illegal" migrant apprehension. In 1882, the Chinese Exclusion Act became the nation's first racist immigration law, banning Chinese laborers from entering the U.S. in addition to denying Chinese immigrants naturalized citizenship.[8] Despite this, Chinese migrants began to enter the U.S. through Mexico, marking an early instance of "illegal" entry. As Patrick Ettinger notes, "By the mid-1920s, [federal authorities] had resigned themselves to creating a border that might serve as a deterrent, rather than a barrier, to undocumented immigrants," such that "the goal of border enforcement, in the words of another federal official, was to 'at least make attempts to cross the border dangerous and to hold illegal entry down to small proportions.'"[9] If, as Brady suggests, Arizona was constituted in misapprehension and if, as Ettinger demonstrates, the geography of the border had already been weaponized to apprehend undocumented immigrants since the 1920s, then a certain juridico-spatial misapprehension between the letter of the law and its material application might have always been the point in border enforcement for more than a century now.

In the twentieth century, the U.S. passed legislation and policy that would dovetail with American civic imaginaries into topoi of a discourse that Leo Chavez identifies as a "Latino threat narrative," even as the U.S. federal government and local businesses recruited foreign labor and produced flows of immigration into the United States.[10] The Immigration Act of 1917 imposed literacy tests on migrants and invented categories of inadmissible subjects under the law. Lisa Flores's analysis of representations of Mexican migrants in public discourse demonstrates how "frequent and persistent characterizations of Mexican migrants as temporary, cheap labor have, in effect, constructed in the cultural imaginary an image of Mexicans as deportable and disposable and racialized them into 'illegality'" as early as the 1920s.[11] Mae Ngai argues that the creation of the Border Patrol invented "illegal" immigration as a rhetorical and juridical form and, additionally, raised the U.S.-Mexico border as a barrier: "During the 1920s immigration policy rearticulated the U.S.-Mexican border as a cultural and racial boundary, as a creator of illegal immigration. Federal officials self-consciously understood their task as creating a barrier where, in a practical sense, none had existed before."[12] The Immigration Act of 1924 constituted the

U.S. Border Patrol (USBP), and the Labor Appropriation Act of 1924 assigned the role of the USBP to police unlawful entry.[13] Kelly Lytle Hernández argues that the USBP did not merely emerge as a reaction to illegal immigration but was a political invention that came to produce, define, and regulate migration in response to racial, economic, and political factors. Hernández argues that USBP practices and policies were instrumental in inventing a racialized and exclusionary regime of policing symptomatic of U.S. nativism and state sovereignty.[14] In the mid-twentieth century, the U.S. experienced an agricultural labor shortage during the Second World War. The Bracero Program (1942–64) recruited more than four million workers, mostly from Mexico, who were expected to leave the U.S. when their work permits expired. Braceros experienced wage theft and dangerous working conditions and were perceived as cheap, temporary workers with no entitlement to citizenship or belonging to U.S. society.[15] "Illegal entrants" became subject to arrest under the law with the Immigration and Nationality Act of 1952. Tens of thousands of migrants were deported to Mexico under Operation Wetback, some of them U.S. citizens. And in 1965, "illegal" immigration took shape as a legal and public commonplace when Congress amended the Immigration and Nationality Act to define numerical limits on immigration from the Western Hemisphere.[16] Legislation in the 1960s, 1980s, and 1990s increasingly criminalized unauthorized immigration and led to the widespread illegalization of migrants, many of whom remained employed in sectors that required their labor.

The Deterrence Era

Facing increasing political pressure to address this putative "Latino threat," President William Clinton wondered in 1993 "what more might be done about the problems along our borders." Clinton concluded, "we must not, and we will not, surrender our borders to those who wish to exploit our history of compassion and justice," and requested $172.5 million for border enforcement, with a substantial budget increase for physical barriers, surveillance technology, and Border Patrol agents.[17] Clinton's budget allocation was influenced by a report that would ultimately usher in a new era of immigration enforcement in the early 1990s.

In 1991, the Office of National Drug Control Policy and the U.S. Immigration and Naturalization Service commissioned Sandia National Laboratories, a federally owned and privately managed laboratory focusing on national security technologies, to complete an analysis of security measures along the U.S.-Mexico border and "to recommend measures by which control of the border could be improved."[18] Sandia issued a report in 1993 titled, "Systematic Analysis of the Southwest Border," which found that "66% of all illegal alien apprehensions occur in 4.7% of the border. That [4.7%] portion is totally contained in two sectors, San Diego and El Paso."[19] Sandia's study suggested that the Border Patrol's traditional methods of immigration enforcement, which were to discourage unlawful entry by apprehending and deporting "illegal aliens" after they entered the United States, was ineffective and reduced the Border Patrol's ability to prevent unlawful entry. Instead, Sandia concluded, Border Patrol should adopt a "prevention" strategy that focused on "imposing effective barriers on the free flow of traffic. . . . The solution is to channel and direct a significantly reduced level of traffic to places where the Border Patrol agents can adequately deal with it."[20]

Sandia's prevention strategy was to control "illegal aliens" by preventing their arrival. Sandia suggested that Border Patrol shore up its resources at major ports of entry like San Diego and El Paso with "heavily patrolled multiple barriers," "24-hour, all-weather highway checkpoints," and information technology like electronic sensors "to count the number of illegal crossings and . . . to feed information into 'intelligent' information control and display systems to alert agents to changes in border traffic patterns and to provide data to more effectively deploy interdiction resources."[21] Sandia notes, for example, that most of the Tucson-sector border "is either mountainous or rugged terrain" that "can be considered natural barrier or traffic channelizer," given that "the terrain in the Tucson sector is very inhospitable, consisting of desert and mountains where daytime summer temperatures regularly exceed 100°F."[22] Concentrated prevention efforts in major ports of entry would be likely to push people to find new border crossing routes in inhospitable terrain where they would be less likely to be apprehended. However, this inhospitable terrain would be used tactically as a natural deterrent: "The ends of the barrier could be located so the Border Patrol could have a significant advantage in that area."[23] The environment itself would be so inhospitable that it would do the work of preventing entry for the Border Patrol.

Sandia's study laid the groundwork for a strategy that INS would adopt and call "Prevention Through Deterrence." In 1994, USBP conceded that "the absolute sealing of the border [was] unrealistic" and, armed with Sandia's study, formalized a strategy of border enforcement it described in a document titled *Border Patrol Strategic Plan 1994 and Beyond.*[24] The document describes deterrence strategy in the following terms:

> The Border Patrol will improve control of the border by implementing a strategy of "prevention through deterrence." The Border Patrol will achieve the goals of its strategy by bringing a decisive number of enforcement resources to bear in each major entry corridor. The Border Patrol will increase the number of agents on the line and make effective use of technology, raising the risk of apprehension high enough to be an effective deterrent. Because the deterrent effect of apprehensions does not become effective in stopping the flow until apprehensions approach 100 percent of those attempting entry, the strategic objective is to maximize the apprehension rate. Although a 100 percent apprehension rate is an unrealistic goal, we believe we can achieve a rate of apprehensions sufficiently high to raise the risk of apprehension to the point that many will consider it futile to continue to attempt illegal entry.[25]

The logic of deterrence is to concentrate enforcement resources on the most heavily trafficked routes of unlawful entry along the U.S.-Mexico border, in San Diego, Nogales, El Paso, and Brownsville, for example, as opposed to spreading enforcement resources across the entire boundary. Fearing apprehension, smugglers and migrants would be dissuaded from entering the U.S. at these heavily fortified areas and instead attempt to cross in significantly more dangerous, hostile terrain that would give the INS the upper hand and increase apprehensions and/or deter migrants from entering: "The prediction is that with traditional entry and smuggling routes disrupted, illegal traffic will be *deterred*, or *forced over* more hostile terrain, less suited for crossing and more suited for enforcement."[26] As Sandia suggested, the strategy marked a significant shift away from previous strategies that focused on apprehending migrants after they had unlawfully entered the United States. Deterrence was mobilized in California in 1994 (Operation Gatekeeper), Texas in 1993 (Operation Hold the Line) and 1997 (Operation Rio Grande), and Arizona in 1999 (Operation Safeguard 99). In San Diego/Tijuana, where migrants and daily commuters alike had crossed the border for more than a hundred years, the U.S. fenced off the international boundary three hundred feet into the Pacific Ocean to the west and to the foothills in the east. Operation Gatekeeper pushed migrants eastward into areas where fencing amounted to little more than barbed wire.

Deterrence has a rhetorical dimension that weaponizes the geography of the Sonoran Desert in California and Arizona (and hostile terrain in New Mexico and Texas) as a commonplace of enforcement. According to a 1996 INS policy document titled *Building a Comprehensive Southwest Border Enforcement Strategy*, "The overarching goal of the strategy is to make it so difficult and so costly to enter this country illegally that fewer individuals even try."[27] The plan was to achieve this by closing off the most traveled routes to divert unlawful entrants through hostile terrain it knew would kill many of them. For example, in a report to Congress in 1999, Richard Stana, director of homeland security and justice issues at the United States Government Accountability Office, noted, "While it does not appear that there has been an increase in the overall number of undocumented migrant deaths, some evidence exists that deaths resulting from attempted crossings in remote areas are increasing, which is an unintended consequence of the strategy."[28] As a transitive verb, "to deter" means "to discourage and turn aside or restrain by fear; to frighten from anything; to restrain or keep back from acting or proceeding by any consideration of danger or trouble" (*Oxford English Dictionary*). To deter is to produce control by rhetorical force in two parts: (1) to *force* migrants to cross over inhospitable terrain by staging the force of law in a militarized spectacle of security at ports of entry that were walled off; (2) to enlist the extreme conditions of the Sonoran Desert as a commonplace of danger in an argument directed at migrants that resonates from the U.S. Border Patrol's 1994 strategic plan through Vice President Kamala Harris's message to migrants at a news conference with Guatemalan President Alejandro Giammattei in 2021: "I want to be clear to folks in this region who are thinking about making that dangerous trek to the United States–Mexico border. Do not come. Do not come. The United States will continue to enforce our laws and secure our border."[29]

Federal officials have argued that deterrence has been successful, evidenced by a decline in apprehensions.[30] Appealing to the effectiveness of deterrence at preventing unlawful entries, U.S. Representative Ed Royce of California had this to say in support of the Secure Fence Act of 2006 (H.R. 6061): "A fair question is, how effective has it been in San Diego? Well, apprehensions along the region with a security fence dropped from 202,000 in 1992 to 9,000 in 1994."[31] In a 2008 press conference with Attorney General Michael Mukasey, Homeland Security Secretary Michael Chertoff spoke in praise of Operation

Streamline, a "zero tolerance" policy mandating federal criminal prosecution of undocumented immigrants caught entering without authorization: "Just in Laredo, in the first 45 days of our Operation Streamline activity there, we saw a reduction in apprehensions of 33 percent. This program works, and the fact that we move it around and focus in on high-tech areas magnifies its deterrent impact."[32] And Jerry Martin, chief of strategic planning and analysis for the USBP, noted that Operation Gatekeeper, for example, "laid important groundwork for Border Patrol's contemporary efforts to achieve operational control of the border. It was a turning point for the Border Patrol."[33] Border Patrol agents were repositioned to the international boundary itself. "Hundreds of unauthorized immigrants would sprint through inspection lanes at the San Ysidro Port of Entry," Martin recalls. "We needed technology to help agents detect illegal activity and additional physical barriers to slow or stop cross-border incursions."[34] A barrier was initially constructed from landing-mat material. And then another layer of landing-mat material was added. Martin recalls the effects of the securitization of the San Ysidrio Port of Entry: "In the years that followed, some chose not to cross, while others attempted to cross in locations with fewer Border Patrol resources. While some may argue this forced individuals to cross through more rugged, dangerous locations, agents stepped up to receive the advanced training required to save lives—no matter a person's immigration status. . . . Our goal is to deter individuals from entering illegally in the first place—not to put them in harm's way."[35] Death would be an incidental and unintended requirement of national security. This wasn't Prevention Through Murder, after all. Regardless of intent, though, Operation Gatekeeper forced migrants eastward into the Sonoran Desert.

This "success," however, is a myth underwritten by a substantial cost to human life. As Douglas Massey argues, the United States created dysfunctional immigration policies in the deterrence era that "have had no detectable effect in deterring undocumented migrants from seeking to come to the United States or in preventing their entry."[36] Migrants haven't stopped trying to cross, and the consequences of deterrence are plain: as of 2024, 4,199 migrants have died while attempting to cross the border through the Sonoran Desert in Arizona alone. Donald Kerwin and Doris Meissner, the latter being the former commissioner of INS from 1993 to 2000, found that even as deterrence-era initiatives "have made it increasingly difficult and dangerous—even life-threatening in some cases—to cross the border illegally," undocumented migrant deaths "continue to loom as a tragic byproduct of border enforcement."[37] Under Meissner, INS reasoned that even if it forced migrants to cross in hostile terrain and they happened to die in the process, it wasn't responsible for their deaths. Deterrence abandoned migrants to a state of exception, exterior to the rule of law, which Giorgio Agamben describes in his landmark study of sovereign power, *Homo Sacer: Sovereign Power and Bare Life*. According to Agamben, sovereignty is grounded in the discursive production of two separate but intimately connected formalizations of life: "Zoe, which expresses the simple fact of living common to all living beings (animals, men, or gods), and *bios*, which indicates the form or way of living proper to an individual or a group."[38] *Bios*, signifying "politically qualified life," does not bear meaning as a self-evident category of life. It is established only through the negative field of *zoe*, a form of life excluded from political order:

> What characterizes modern politics is not so much the inclusion of *zoe* in the polis. . . . Instead the decisive fact is that, together with the process by which the exception everywhere becomes the rule, the realm of bare life— which is originally situated at the margins of the political order—gradually begins to coincide with the political realm, and exclusion and inclusion, outside and inside, *bios* and *zoe*, right and fact, enter into a zone of irreducible indistinction. At once excluding bare life from and capturing it within the political order, the state of exception actually constituted, in its very separateness, the hidden foundation on which the entire political system rested.[39]

Federal officials in 1920s had acknowledged a spatial crisis constitutive of U.S. sovereignty, staged by the border's irreducible porosity.[40] Deterrence is the latest entry in an index of more than a century's worth of racist discursive practice, which now produces undocumented migrant subjectivity as bare life: one who is indeed included within the order of the law, insofar as migrants are allowed to be killed with impunity, but also simultaneously excluded from it, insofar as their deaths count as neither homicide nor sacrifice. INS abandoned migrants to a space of lawlessness, physically and discursively interior to the United States but beyond its domain in a subject position that Lisa Cacho calls "social death."[41] Legally, INS couldn't deliberately kill migrants; however, it could allow them to die in a "non-place" of hostile terrain.[42] If migrants fell into harm's way crossing the desert, as Martin reasons, agents would try their damnedest to save them. But the U.S. wouldn't be responsible for migrant deaths if migrants made the choice to try to cross in hostile terrain—even if the U.S. persuaded them to make that choice with the rhetorical force of deterrence. Migrants, reduced to bare life, don't reside outside civic space but intimately within it as its constitutive exteriority. "Illegal" immigration is at once a topos around which sovereign power organizes itself and the excess of its domain.

In the deterrence era, lost migrants are not an accidental consequence of border enforcement—they are its condition of possibility. Mary Fan argues that the "borderlands are not a state of exception in Agamben's specific sense of a place where law is *suspended*." Fan concludes that migrants are not reduced to bare life, as there are laws that subject those who would seek to harm migrants to criminal and civil sanctions; instead, Fan argues, migrants are reduced to *basic* life without "entitlements that make the good life sweet."[43] Perhaps this is hair-splitting, but I think Fan and I read this issue from different angles. Consider that Scott Warren, who worked with the humanitarian aid organization No Más Muertes in Tucson, Arizona, was put on trial by federal prosecutors for aiding two undocumented migrants at a humanitarian aid station known as The Barn. Warren was acquitted. But federal prosecutor Michael Bailey argued in court that Warren was complicit in human trafficking and told NPR, "We won't distinguish between whether someone is harboring or trafficking for money or whether they're doing it out of a misguided sense of social justice or belief in open borders."[44] After Warren's acquittal, he still faced a misdemeanor charge, eventually dismissed in 2020, of driving on a restricted road in the Cabeza Prieta National Wildlife Refuge to drop off water and food for migrants in a remote area of the desert. Warren's case exemplifies just how punitive the federal government has become in maintaining its efforts to dehumanize migrants beyond civic life at all.

The U.S.-Mexico border wall, in its porosity, stages an ongoing shift in sovereignty. The United States is positioned above the law, suspended to the degree that the state and Sandia are not subject to the law and cannot be held responsible for its policies that continue to kill undocumented migrants. Undocumented migrants are allowed to be killed with impunity even if the law prevents U.S. citizens from killing them. Even if the law is not suspended for the members of The Minutemen Project, it is suspended for undocumented migrants and the sovereign federal government alike. Additionally, within the commonplace of security that characterizes the rhetorical terrain of U.S. immigration policy in the deterrence era, the wall is chiasmus: as a topos indexing the spatial distinctions on which sovereignty hinges, the wall cannot

MISAPPREHENSION   33

but simultaneously serve to index the disintegrating distinctions between friend and enemy, inside and out, and law and lawlessness. The U.S.-Mexico border wall and the negative spaces of "hostile terrain" where there are few walls stage the "complete operational control" of sovereign territory that it cannot exercise. The wall is a topos of sovereign law and security even as it produces the lawlessness and death it is supposed to prevent through deterrence.

Misapprehension

Deterrence weaponizes the desert as a topos (as atopos), harnessing the geography of this extreme terrain as a rhetorical force. The Tucson sector of the Border Patrol runs 261 miles from the Yuma county line, just east of Dateland in map 1, to New Mexico along the international boundary between the United States and Mexico. This stretch of the U.S.-Mexico border cuts through the Sonoran Desert, which can heat up to 118 degrees Fahrenheit in the summers and whose land surface temperature has been observed to reach 177.44 Fahrenheit, one of the highest land surface temperatures ever recorded.[45] The Sonoran Desert has a reputation as a site of extreme danger. According to Todd Miller, "More people began crossing through places such as the Arizona desert. The places are so dangerous, desolate, and deadly that the hostile terrain itself, according to Border Patrol's 'prevention by deterrence' strategy, is supposed to stop prospective migrants in their tracks. This did not jibe with Mexico's post-NAFTA exodus, in which historic numbers of people began journeying to the United States—often through terrain where it was impossible to carry even enough clean water necessary for the three-day trek. The region is literally littered with bones."[46]

Estimates suggest that more than six million people have attempted to cross into the United States through this sector.[47] Thousands have died in the attempt. According to the *Mapa de Migrantes Fallecidos*, 4,199 migrant remains have been recovered. A report from the Binational Migration Institute at the University of Arizona suggests that USBP has underreported the number of migrant deaths in its own official count by as much as 50 percent: "Beginning in 2014, PCOME cases began to exceed estimates reported by Border Patrol, and in recent years, have done so by as much as two-fold. Given this divergence since 2014, we caution readers against relying on US Border Patrol recovered UBC remains estimates for the Tucson Sector in order to generalize about migrant deaths in southern Arizona."[48] Another report, issued by La Coalición

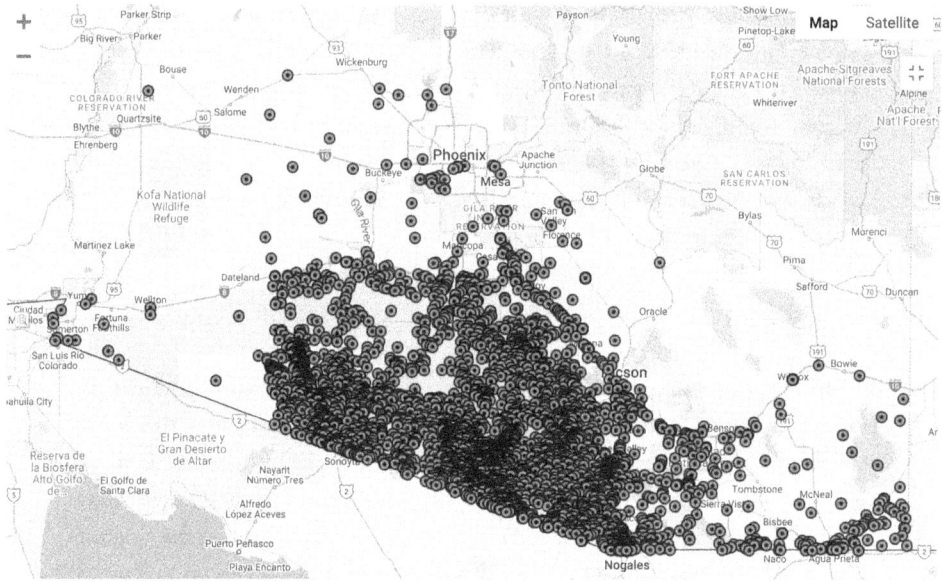

Map 1 | The *Mapa de Migrantes Fallecidos*, a digital map maintained by the Pima County Office of the Medical Examiner and Humane Borders, shows the locations of more than four thousand migrant deaths in southern Arizona. Each red dot represents one set of migrant remains recovered between 1990 and 2024. Human Borders.

de Derechos Humanos and No Más Muertes, two Tucson-based advocacy groups, notes, "we cannot know the total number of lives lost in the border-lands; the region has been transformed into a vast graveyard of the missing."[49]

In contemporary debates over immigration, it has become commonplace for advocates of migrant hospitality to express how little is known about the true extent of the crisis of human rights at the U.S.-Mexico border and, in turn, how this lack of knowledge forecloses on the possibility for practical reasoning to inform policy change. Rob O'Dell, Daniel González, and Jill Castellano argue, for example, that "the lack of a full accounting of border deaths diminishes the full impact of the humanitarian crisis [and] deprives policymakers of informa-tion that could save lives, through enforcement efforts or changes to immigra-tion laws."[50] I wonder, however, if this is a situation in which practical reasoning is possible, let alone the right tool to use. What reason do we have to believe that more accurate accounts of migrant deaths will lead to more humane immigra-tion policy and enforcement? I'm less sure now than ever that a better apprehen-sion of undocumented migrancy will ever lend itself to practical reasoning that would somehow humanize migrants to those who would be unwilling (or perhaps unable) to grant them the basic human dignity that would serve as the condition of possibility for their access to human rights, let alone citizenship. To belabor this point, consider a letter written to *The Arizona Republic* in response to a USA Today Network investigation, which found that the USBP had undercounted the number of migrants who died passing through the Sonoran Desert: "American taxpayers are supposed to feel obligated to finance the gathering and identification of the remains. Not only that, American taxpayers are supposed to gather around and go boo-hoo and wring their hands over the deaths of these criminals. I have a request to make of those mourners who want to tell me how sad it is that criminal invaders of my country died in their criminal effort. Go directly to hell. Do not pass GO. Do not collect anything."[51]

We will never know the full extent of the U.S.'s abuses of the human rights of undocumented migrants. I want to unpack what this means. In a denotative sense, it means that a better understanding of this crisis (in the possession of more or better data in, say, exact death counts and identification of human remains) isn't available. Not right now, at least. Connotatively, I'm skeptical that a better understanding, grounded in more accurate and complete data, would serve to humanize undocumented migrants to federal officials and the author of the letter just quoted. I'm skeptical that a full accounting of border deaths would put an end to the needless and ongoing fatalities of undocumented migrants. After all, deterrence was designed with this outcome in mind. And even as research from the Vera Institutive of Justice in 2018 demonstrates, for example, that "there is no evidence to support the conclusion that Operation Streamline succeeded in deterring unauthorized border crossings, nor that it had any effect whatsoever on immigrants' decisions to come to the United States," public rhetorics about immigration remain saturated in appeals to criminalize undocumented migrants.[52] If this is the case, then we might contend with the possibility that the archaeological truth about the extent and scale of this crisis, *even if* it were available, might never serve as a topos (a storehouse of social energy) from which to harvest rhetorical energy to invent a just immigration policy.

Nevertheless, there is a deterritorializing quality in this topical impasse, a *misapprehensive* dimension of deterrence, excessive to itself and archived in the *Mapa de Migrantes Fallecidos*: 37 percent, or 1,560, of the 4,199 recovered human remains are named as "unidentified." Even as the *Mapa de Migrantes Fallecidos* archives information about *los migrantes fallecidos*, it also archives what isn't yet known (identities of unidentified remains), what might still yet be known (the possibility of restituting unidentified remains with an identity), and what might never be known at all. The *Mapa de Migrantes Fallecidos* identifies some victims with a proper name, but it will probably never fully apprehend and restitute proper names to all recovered human remains. It archives a possibility of a thought of *los migrantes fallecidos* that is incalculable, beyond any possibility of apprehension. While it can be mined to invent arguments supporting any side of the dispute about immigration policy, the *Mapa de Migrantes Fallecidos* is also marked by a counterpart to its potential for rhetorical invention, or perhaps an exorbitant and unintended counterpart, that can't lead to apprehension (in the simultaneous sense of arrest and understanding) but nevertheless has a deterritorializing effect in the form of a misapprehension. This misapprehension in the text does not establish a topos for a practical reasoning other than as a position that cannot provide the desire for truth with rhetorical force and, therefore, cannot be enlisted to enforce truth. I provisionally name this misapprehensive excess as a motif of rhetorical disinvention—an emergent and exorbitant semiosis incapable of force that holds open a possibility for thought of *los migrantes fallecidos* beyond the will to apprehend.

I read this misapprehension as a rhetoricity of hospitality that would stand in contrast to what Derrida identified in *Rogues* as "the reason of the strongest." Derrida reads Jean La Fontaine's fable "The Wolf and the Lamb" to allegorize the question of the relation between law and force. In the fable, a wolf invents reasons to prey on a lamb drinking downstream. The wolf initially accuses the lamb of muddying the water, which is impossible. After the lamb refutes this accusation, the wolf invents another reason, this time in the form of an accusation of slander from the previous year. The lamb, only months old, cannot possibly be guilty of this charge either. Regardless of the lamb's defense, the wolf reasons that the blame must fall on the lamb's family, thereby "justifying" its attack. Is the lesson here that might overpowers right, as the fable is commonly read? Perhaps the fable narrativizes something more: that law presupposes its enforcement through a coercive, violent force that it launders as reason.[53] Derrida suggests that for law to be recognized as legitimate, it must be grounded in a force—a "mystical" violence that legitimizes the law even as it cannot be fully rationalized within the grammar of the law itself. It is "mystical" because its origins and legitimacy are excessive to the language of law, suggesting that the authority of law is based more on a commonplace acceptance of its legitimacy than on any rational or ethical foundation. The fable narrativizes the capacity of reason to become a commonplace for justifying the oppression of the weak by the strong and challenges the notion of reason as a neutral, universal zero coordinate of justice. What is considered reasonable often reflects the interests and worldview of the "strongest," the people in authority, illustrating the arbitrary nature of justifications for dominance.

The fable also narrativizes a weakness in reason when faced with the force of might, which comes not from a lack of rationality but from a misfire in reason and its application. This weakness is not merely a limitation but a trace of an emergent semiosis that is irreducible to the force of law. Whereas law consists of codified rules for governing society, justice marks a rhetoricity constitutive of, and always deferred beyond, any legal code. Laws are enforceable; justice is not. Instead, justice is marked by a weak "force" in comparison to the force of law, an unenforceability, an infinitely unconditional openness irreducible to any legal code underwriting sovereign authority: a "force without power [that] opens up unconditionally to what or who *comes* and comes to affect it."[54] It would be incompatible with any force of reason used by the strongest over the weakest. This weak force would be incompatible, for example, with policing: "No politics, no ethics, and no law can be, as it were, *deduced* from this thought. To be sure, nothing can be *done* [*faire*] with it."[55] Nothing could be done with this weak force; it couldn't be recovered and used by any political party as a strong force of reason. From the exorbitant rhetoricity of *los migrantes fallecidos*, we bear witness to the impossibility of apprehending, of knowing, as the grounds of rhetoric. We encounter, in turn, a will to misapprehend as an unsettling rhetoricity.

2

Displacement | Rhetorical Invention and Decoloniality

The difficult task is not to enlarge the content and to be more inclusive but rather to reconfigure the parameters of the debate.
—Walter Mignolo, *The Darker Side of the Renaissance: Literacy, Territoriality, and Colonization*

In *The Darker Side of the Renaissance: Literacy, Territoriality, and Colonization* (1998), Walter Mignolo argues that the discourse of modernity couldn't have been invented without the obscured grounding of the European Renaissance that preceded it. In addition to its intellectual and cultural achievements, the Renaissance marked "the rebirth of the classical tradition as a justification of colonial expansion."[1] In Mignolo's reading, the European Renaissance itself became a commonplace for justifying colonial expansion in Latin America. History, furthermore, is often narrated from a European "locus of enunciation" (epistemic standpoint) assumed to be both objectively true and universal. It is problematic, Mignolo reasons, "to 'think' from the canon of Western philosophy, even when part of the canon is critical of modernity. To do so means to reproduce the blind epistemic ethnocentrism that makes difficult, if not impossible, any political philosophy of inclusion."[2] In other words, it's time to "think" from beyond the commonplaces of Western modernity.

This premise has become resonant in rhetorical studies, as prior discussions about accounting for alterity in rhetorical histories have found new ground in rhetorical studies' recent decolonial turn. Three passages serve as examples: (1) Damián Baca details a historiographic tendency in the field to formalize Western writing cultures as the origin point and apex of a Eurocentric narrative of rhetorical history. This "enduring Aristotelian syndrome," which he describes as "the rhetorical art of reinventing the cultural Other as a periphery that is declared as such from the colonizing center," drives a historiographical essentialism that reads the Americas as the preliterate and, therefore, inferior Western exteriority.[3] On account of this, Baca argues, "comparative rhetorics should not erase the complex differences between contrastive civilizations by using European descriptions of Western rhetorical practice as a universal frame for understanding diverse cultural traditions in Mesoamerica."[4] (2) Darrel Wanzer-Serrano "[refuses] to normalize a Eurocentric narrative of Western civilization that anchors Greece and Rome as the cornerstone of 'Western thought,'" by "[being] attentive to the locatedness of that knowledge and [resisting] reproducing a 'zero point epistemology' that crowds out alternate knowledges." Noting that rhetorical theory can be "rooted in problematic assumptions," Wanzer-Serrano proposes to delink rhetoric from coloniality by "[naming] and [recognizing] limits of location."[5] (3) Abraham Romney suggests situating rhetorical history in the colonial periphery, arguing that such a relocation helps "U.S.-based rhetoricians to see the field from the other side of the street." While he brackets this claim, noting that "the relationship to rhetoric exercised by those marginalized by rhetoric is not simply that of exclusion," he proposes a locational thinking, which he speculates could help rhetorical studies "adopt an ethical approach that views the field from its margins to ensure that rhetoric's colonizing past" does "not give way to an imperial future."[6]

But how exactly do appeals to locational and cultural difference produce egalitarian political and epistemological changes? I think that what is at stake in decoloniality is homologous to the stakes of a question Christa Olson posed: "Is the idea of 'rhetoric' itself irredeemably place-bound?"[7] I want to build on Olson's question to ask, Is the idea of rhetoric irredeemably commonplace-bound? Does one's epistemic standpoint determine the meaning and truth of what one says? Is it valid to assume that the physical and/or social location from which one issues or receives speech determines the form and content of what one can say and hear? When, and to what degree, is it valid for me to speak for or about (to represent) someone different from me? Is alterity place-bound—does it signify from somewhere? If not, how are we to read rhetoric that takes place *without* location, issued from subjects whose part in a rhetorical situation is defined by not having one? In this chapter, I consider how the stakes of disinvention foreshadow the eclipse of decoloniality as a topos of rhetorical and political thought and, in turn, plot an exigence for moving past decoloniality without completely giving up on it. My wager is that such questions will contribute to a rhetorical historiography that prompts a rhetoricity of hospitality otherwise than grids of intelligibility produced by deterrence.

Poligraphy

Questions about the stakes of cultural difference have become commonplace in rhetorical studies. In recent years, critics have pointed this question at emerging postnational realities in the United States, where the increasing passage of people across national boundaries has become symptomatic of changes to more traditional and stable sites of identification.[8] Just a few years after rhetoricians discussed writing pluralist histories of rhetoric in the landmark "Octalog: The Politics of Historiography" (1988) transcript, for example, the Latin American Subaltern Studies Group (LASSG) published a statement (1994) summarizing the challenges of writing historiographies in times marked by a crisis in models of hegemony.[9] In the statement, the LASSG founders observe, "The redefinition of Latin American political and cultural space in recent years has . . . impelled scholars of the region to revise established and previously functional epistemologies in the social sciences and humanities."[10] To what degree scholars have been impelled to revise previously functional epistemologies amid the ongoing crisis in models of hegemony has been the subject of debate across fields over the past thirty years.

Since at least the first Octalog, scholars have maintained an ongoing inquiry about how to perceive rhetorical expressions that will have been different from what counts as rhetoric in a Western rhetorical tradition. James J. Murphy writes in the Octalog that whereas politics is "the examination of how communities work toward their commonly perceived goods," the historiographer of rhetoric is "a grapher of the *polis*," one who accounts for "what ought to be discovered for the good of the community."[11] In the same conversation, Robert J. Connors writes, "I write history to try to make my world a better place. . . . And in order to do this at all, I have to accept certain things in my epistemological world, as assented to by you, by people who read what I write, by the community of discourse in which I live. I have to accept the idea that truth for us is consensually created by our assent to it."[12] Whose world will Connors try to make a better place when he writes history? Even as the "I" (writer) and the "you" (reader) serve as constitutive fictions of rhetorical theory, there is a conflation of pronouns from the first sentence (I try to make *my* world a better place) to the third ("truth for *us* is consensually created by *our* assent to it"). The supplementation of the "I" with the "us" is irreducible here. We, as audience, are already hailed into Connors's world despite our consent, though given that his world is defined by a community that always already assumes "us." For Connors, caught between the "I" and the "us" as the effect of writing history, writing history means informally representing that to which "all of us" have yet to consent. At best, "our" consent will come after history has been written.

Poligraphy is a historiographical practice that turns on an irreducible indistinction between "I" and "all," such that a polygrapher always speaks on behalf of all. If, in Murphy's terms, the grapher of the polis, *poligrapher*, documents how communities work toward their commonly perceived goods, and if the sign *community* marks an improper noun without a proper referent (after all, by definition, "community" never refers to any one specific individual but an assemblage of individuals), then the poligrapher serves as an informal representative for commonly perceived intellectual goods in a heterogeneous group of people, all of whom hold different perceptions of what *ought* to be discovered. But how, and to what degree, can one speak about others who are not like me? And what are the conditions that determine how different I am from others? Can a white poligrapher, for example, speak for a community that includes nonwhite people?

In 1991, just a few years after the first Octalog, the philosopher Linda Martín Alcoff framed the problem of speaking for others as one presupposing a relation between speech and location. Alcoff notes that the problem of speaking for others arises from two premises: first, "a speaker's location is epistemically salient."[13] As Alcoff notes, it is too often assumed that the location from which one speaks determines one's capacity for speech. It is not merely that it affects the meaning and truth of one's speech but that one's location determines the meaning of their speech. Location (meaning one's social location, subject position) "has an epistemically significant impact on that speaker's claims and can serve to either authorize or disauthorize one's speech."[14] This first premise is essentially a question of ethos, of how, and to what degree, one's location bears on meaning.

The second premise is "not only is location epistemically salient, but certain privileged locations are discursively dangerous." Alcoff asks, "Is it ever valid to speak for others who are unlike me or who are less privileged than me?"[15] The question prompts yet another question for rhetorical studies: On what criteria can we ground definitions of identity or membership in groups to mark differences between self and other implied in the problem of speaking for others? Another question unfolds from there: If the practice of speaking for others is problematic, can one simply speak *about* others instead? Further, would one be abdicating their political responsibility to speak truth to power by staying silent so that those who are less privileged can speak on their own terms? No matter the place from which one speaks (be it about self or other, groups one formally represents or groups one only informally represents), if the practice of speaking *for* others is problematic, then so is the practice of speaking *about* others, since both practices represent, or construct, the subject position of the other. If the problem of speaking for others is a problem of misrepresentation, whereby the consequences of misrepresentation constitute violence and dehumanization, then perhaps it would be possible to retreat from representation and instead listen to the other, as some folks in rhetorical studies have suggested.[16] The problem here is that in the attempt to foreclose misrepresentation—by listening (whereby listening means not representing) instead of speaking (representing)—the act of listening is assumed to be nonideological because it is not engaged in representation (speaking). However, there is no location from which to speak that is disentangled from the discursive structures that ground others. One cannot only speak for themselves, in other words, so the solution to the problem of speaking for others cannot be found in only speaking about oneself or the categories one formally represents.

Let's return to Connors's desire to "to make my world a better place." In this phrase, "my" cannot but simultaneously signify "our," for we all share a world with Connors whether we choose to or not. When it comes to representing one's world, the distance between "mine" and "our" will always be irreducible even if there is an implied or explicitly stated subject. We learned this lesson in the twentieth century when dictators across Latin America and Europe declared their intent to make the world a better place without defining for whom exactly that world would be better. Still, the question of how communities perceive what is common remains somewhat nebulous. This presupposition about what is common, about how what is common is perceived, will drive the question of historiography through three more Octalogs and counting. Murphy writes, "the place where one stands will have a great influence on what the historian's lever can move."[17] It is this relation between place and speech (logos) on which the disagreement over plurality in the rhetorical tradition turns. In fact, what we see here is that the first Octalog recirculated a common disagreement, one in which comparative rhetoricians of Latin America will ground their arguments twenty years later.

Locus of Enunciation

While rhetorical scholarship of Latin America is relatively nascent, much of the scholarship is grounded Walter Mignolo's work on decoloniality, whose concept of locus of enunciation has become a cornerstone for rereading the legacies of coloniality across the region. In this section, I offer a reading of this critical concept. I argue that when viewed from my reading of this concept, claims about decolonization across comparative rhetorical studies will appear to be less egalitarian than they are currently assumed to be. This, I argue, establishes an exigence to revisit and rethink the theoretical foundations that shape comparativist inquiry across fields. In this sense, I believe rhetorical studies has a contribution to make to Latin American studies after importing its ideas for so long.

In *The Darker Side of the Renaissance*, Mignolo argues that there is reason to historicize Western modernity from the 1492 colonization of the Americas instead of from the Enlightenment in later centuries, for by the sixteenth century, missionaries from Spain were already assessing the humanity of Indigenous peoples in the Americas on whether they possessed alphabetic writing and, later, whether they possessed history. Mignolo reads, in the missionaries' claims about humanity and writing, a commonplace of difference that would become a well of social energy and moral grounding for an assemblage of legal, philosophical, political, and cultural discourse that scholars now historiographically call Western modernity. Building on Enrique Dussel, who argues that modernity is "a European phenomenon, but one constituted in a dialectical relation with a non-European alterity that is its ultimate content," Mignolo argues that Western modernity's metanarrative constitutes itself from an occluded commonplace of *colonial difference*: an alterity that is also its most interior condition of possibility.[18] There is reason, therefore, to investigate this assumed colonial difference because its rhetorical force locates Western modernity as the universal zero coordinate of truth:

> The entire sphere of knowledge, of modern knowledge, was constituted assuming a "cero point" and an epistemic privilege that materialized in philosophy and, above all, in science. The "cero-point" was at once local as

a locus of enunciation and global as locus of the enunciated, since it was the only historical "cero-point" in conditions to account for the entire planet, to "integrate" the diversality of the planet to the universality of the "cero-point" of observation. In other words, the "cero point" *incorporates* the diverse within its sameness and epistemic homogeneity at the same time that it *expels* the diverse to the colonial difference (epistemic above all, described from the perspective of the "cero point" as religious, linguistic, and "cultural" differences).[19]

Mignolo's argument critiques a commonplace framing of Western modernity as the universal *and* originary location of truth. In this book, this is what I understand "Eurocentrism" to signify. Not only did Spanish missionaries presuppose that Indigenous people lacked possession of logos in lacking literacy, Mignolo argues that the Spaniards presupposed alphabetic literacy as the measuring stick of civilization. But it's not simply a matter of miscommunication across linguistic or cultural difference, as Jon Beasley-Murray reminds us. Beasley-Murray notes an instance in the writing of Bartolomé de las Casas, in which, after learning about the prospect of gold in a given town, Spanish conquistadors performed the Requerimiento ritual at night and out of earshot of the Native peoples before setting fire to the town. The Requerimiento ritual wasn't performed to communicate: "The native inhabitants can neither accept nor reject the choice that the Spaniards offer. They are beyond the pale of any possible community."[20] Instead, Mignolo argues that neither communication nor translation is available across this constitutive *colonial difference* simply because one does not translate into speech the noise emanating from those "newly discovered" peoples. In speaking about Indigenous peoples of the Americas, Spanish missionaries were not simply always already speaking for them; instead, there was no stage for a dispute to be had because they had already dispossessed Indigenous peoples of the logos and, in turn, themselves of an interlocutor.

Mignolo's reading here follows a prior line of reasoning that Alcoff had separately developed genealogically with Gayatri Spivak's reading of subalternity. "The influential question asked several years ago by Gayatri Spivak," Mignolo notes, "was 'Can the subaltern speak?'" The question "could be answered by saying that the subaltern have always spoken, although scholars and social scientists were not always willing to listen." That is, "*the question of whether the colonized can be represented may no longer be an issue*, and it could be reframed in terms of dialogues from different loci of enunciation rather than as an academic mono-logue performed in the act of 'studying' colonial discourse and not 'listening' to politically engaged persons (whether inside or out-side academe), writers from colonial, postcolonial, or Third World countries producing alternative dis-course."[21] Whereas Alcoff argues that the problem of speaking for (representing) others is unavoidable, Mignolo here suggests that the problem of representing (speaking for) the colonized might not be an issue if academics would just listen instead of speaking, or avoid representation altogether in favor of what he calls "enactment." Mignolo describes this alternative as avoiding the problems associ-ated with representation that Spivak so carefully articulates in "Can the Subal-tern Speak?": "Representation is a notion I have tried to avoid as much as possible in my argument. If I say that I was interested in how European peoples and communities constructed the idea of the self-same instead of in how they 'repre-sented the other,' it is because my interests are located more in enactment than in representation."[22] I recognize that the spirit of Mignolo's argument is to ulti-mately pluralize the right to speak and be heard beyond academic traditions of studying outsiders. I also want to sit with one of the premises of Mignolo's con-cept of enactment, which is that it is possible to hear subaltern speech at all. Enactment would be impassive because enacting the non-Western subaltern subject would have the effect of universalizing colonial difference in a most West-ern fashion: enactment turns not simply on the pluralization of truth but also on the truth of pluralization—it is premised in the possibility of an absolute, uni-versal representation that can be known and communicated (pluralization). This wouldn't be a problem except that Mignolo's thesis is opposed to universalism.

Mignolo's critique of Eurocentric modernity is a critique of representation *in general*. For Mignolo, the path forward is to develop knowledge from a subaltern perspective—from a locus of enunciation outside of Eurocentric modernity to provincialize Eurocentric modernity's zero point function. At this point, Migno-lo's argument pivots to commonplaces of exteriority and exceptionalism.[23] This is confirmed early in *The Darker Side of the Renaissance*, when Mignolo considers the relation between speech and the location from which it is issued: "If post-modern and postcolonial are suspicious expressions either because we are not out of modernity or colonialism or because by using them the preference that modernity attributes to time over space is reinforced, I would like to emphasize that, in spite of all the ambiguities, postmodernity and postcoloniality designate (in my argument) the locations of two different modes of countering modernity.

If 'deconstruction' is a mode or operation associated with the former, 'decoloniza-tion' is the corresponding one associated with the latter."[24] What exactly is the nature of this difference between two different modes of countering modernity? Location. Conceptually, locus of enunciation refers to both social/epistemic and physical locations that shape meaning and truth in speech issued from them. Mignolo's thesis reads this difference as the exigence for developing new reading practices from a locus of enunciation beyond Eurocentric modernity, which he later refers to as "[an] other logic (or border thinking *from the perspective of subal-ternity*) . . . that regionalizes the fundamental European legacy, locating thinking in the colonial difference and creating the conditions for diversality as a universal project."[25] If such a difference is established on the grounds of location (that is, the impropriety of European ideas in describing speech issued from in Latin America), then what appears to qualify postcolonial speech as "decolonial" is in it being an exception to the example of Eurocentric modernity.[26]

Decolonizing Rhetorical Invention

In recent years, scholars of Latinx and Latin American rhetorics, for example, have argued that it's not enough to informally represent those whose voices will have been different from the Western rhetorical tradition. I underscore the importance for Indigenous and Latinx people to self-represent their place in a rhetorical tradition. Still, this proposed location for formally representing a Latin American locus of enunciation is a fiction of Western modernity that simply cannot confirm an exteriority to it; instead, this topos of "the Americas" is the very constitutive interiority of Western modernity itself. I'm unconvinced that theories of pluralism can't be thought from within Western modernity.

An important articulation of topical theory inspired by Mignolo's locus of enunciation is Damián Baca and Victor Villanueva's *Rhetorics of the Americas, 3114 BCE to 2012 CE* (2010), the field's first edited collection of essays on rhe-torical discourse in Latin America. Framed as a volume of scholarship on a "uniquely Western Hemispheric" Indigenous rhetorical discourse, *Rhetorics of the Americas* advances a set of claims regarding the stakes of rewriting rhetori-cal historiography from the perspective of the Americas—that is, from the assumed consciousness of rhetorical forms that emerge from uniquely Ameri-can space.[27] The collection, in other words, makes an explicit move to include

analyses on texts and writers from beyond the boundaries of hegemonic European perspectives and specifically from an assumed Indigenous consciousness.
Additionally, this disciplinary intervention sets out to challenge the predomi-
nance of European and U.S.-American based narratives in critical debates on
writing in Latin America.

In the opening essay of the collection, Baca describes the dynamics at work in
the conception of a uniquely non-Western space. Although the given objective of
the collection is to fill an epistemological gap by providing a more rigorous
understanding of "rhetoric that coincided with but was not influenced by Greco-
Roman inventions" to describe "the invention of the Americas" as a colonial
invention,[28] Baca simultaneously posits an exceptional location of culture from
which to advance claims about the limits of Western reason:

> Ultimately, accounting for historically grounded voices and communica-
> tive practices promotes a more inclusive and historically sound theory of
> how rhetoric is and has been practiced across regions, cultures, and migra-
> tions unique to the Americas and the Caribbean. Accounting for such prac-
> tices, further, provides more accurate understandings of how indigenous
> artists and writers have responded and continue to respond to imperialist
> teleology and Western expansion. Urging scholars away from the sources
> that reinforce Eurocentric perspectives of Pre-Columbian history, this
> collection advances a revision of colonial images of the Americas that have
> continued over the last 500 years. Focusing on rhetoric outside of the
> dominant and virtually exclusive Greco-Latin canon, our contributors
> look to the practices and traditions unique to Mesoamerica, México,
> Guatemala, Peru, Boriquén, Hawai'i, and the U.S./México borderlands,
> among other places within the Western Hemisphere.[29]

Here, the rhetorics of the Americas are framed as an emergent form that has
two important defining qualities: they are uniquely *American* (which is to say,
not European and therefore *not* Eurocentric), and because of this exceptional
quality, they are linked to the radicalism involved with resistance to Western
imperialist reason. Baca goes on to present the formula of hemispheric American rhetorical criticism as political reflection ("a more inclusive and historically
sound theory") grounded in ideas of cultural difference and authenticity ("the
practices and traditions unique to Mesoamerica, México, Guatemala, Peru,

Boriquén, Hawai'i, and the U.S./México borderlands") that serve to restitute social groups ("rhetoric outside of the dominant and virtually exclusive Greco-Latin canon") that have been excluded from the histories of speech and politics. In other words, it is this very exceptional locus of enunciation that is taken to be the grounds for resisting the universalization of hegemonic European discourse. Ultimately, this critique depends on sharp geopolitical disjunctions (interior/exterior, center/periphery) that posit the local as representing resistance to a non-American metropole. One is advised, therefore, to recognize that there are two modes of reading this geopolitical boundary: an ideological mode that reinforces "Eurocentric perspectives of Pre-Columbian history" and a nonideological mode that does not. From this vantage, the rhetorics of the Americas form an exceptional locus of uniquely American rhetorical production that is simultaneously the exemplary confirmation of European discourse and the exception from it.

Baca's theory of an exterior and resistant American semiosis in conjunction with Mignolo's locus of enunciation has come to constitute a major theoretical disposition for analyzing non-Western rhetorical activity in the region. However, this presupposition of difference remains mostly uninterrogated. Additionally, Cristina Ramírez claims that in order to "expand our field's understanding of how to conduct research into non-Western rhetorics," one must enact a unique, authentic Latin American form of subjectivity and consciousness: mestizaje.[30] Ramírez advances this idea of an exceptionally Latin American racial and cultural quality—which, she claims, is "grounded in the identity and actions of the mother of the mestizo race, Malintzin"—to articulate a reading of mestiza rhetorics as a subversive "decolonizing approach to identification outside of the dominant narrative of assimilation" that "breaks with the tired trope of well-known Euro-and malecentric stories" by providing "an authentic connection with [Mexico's] past." "With the re/visioned history and rhetorical actions of Malintzin at its core," she argues, "mestiza rhetoric can represent this symbolic puesto by calling on indigenous cultural symbols and knowledge, representing an intertextuality of cultures and ideas, while resisting assimilation to a linear articulation of logic, thereby resulting in divergent, subversive texts."[31]

Ramírez establishes a familiar example/exception binary (Europe/Mexico) opposition as the means for removing the totalizing grounds of Eurocentrism's "linear articulation of logic" and relocating the production of history to a mestiza *puesto* (locus of enunciation). Having flattened these loci to place them on more egalitarian grounds, Ramírez is now able to assert the exceptional and heterogeneous quality of mestizaje that operates "outside of the dominant narrative of assimilation." However in the move to articulate the exceptional quality of mestizaje's difference from Eurocentrism, Ramírez appeals to the topoi of race and nativism associated with Mexico's "authentic past." Additionally, in the same way that Mignolo abandons representation in favor of enacting the authentic subaltern consciousness as a semiosis of resistance, Ramírez wagers that one must enact "an ontological shift" by listening to the voices of marginalized rhetors so that one may "liberate the free play of differences." Yet she hedges this bet, noting that "theories from scholars in the United States are different from theories of mestizaje from Mexico because of the authors' geographic and ethnic positions."[32] In her attempt to prevent mestizaje from being absorbed into the "dominant narrative of assimilation," Ramírez invokes the very topoi of essentialism (racial difference, nativism) ascribed to non-Western cultures.

Indeed, this impasse marks a need for new ways of thinking in postnational times. If, as Abraham Romney suggests, the Western tradition has ceased to be the privileged location for the production and representation of culture and if, as Mignolo indicates, political and cultural forces have long functioned in a way that undermines the model of Western superiority and if, as Baca notes, the partition of Western and non-Western spaces produces locations from which to critique Western epistemological hegemony, then perhaps we are no longer able to think cultural difference from exclusively within the established boundaries of Western concepts. However, it is equally possible that these reflections indicate the waning of stable borders, subjectivities, and locations in general.

While there are some important differences characterizing various decolonial projects, they nonetheless share grounding in a very specific assumption about the relationship between location and politics. As Mignolo puts it, "The limit of Western philosophy is the border where the colonial difference emerges, making visible the variety of local histories that Western thought, from the right and the left, hid and suppressed."[33] The warrant, here, is an absolute relation between location and knowledge or, more precisely, that location is constitutive of knowledge (coloniality : modernity :: location : knowledge). It is from this presupposition regarding the politics of location, in other words, that the various projects of decoloniality conflate the topos of Latin American with the topos of borderlands as topoi of resistance to Western modernity: "Border thinking is the epistemology of the exteriority; that is, of the outside created from the inside; and as such, it is always a decolonial project."[34] Implied here is the location borderlands as an exterior to the Western canon from which to think the field of the political outside the terms and conditions of Western hegemony, figured through the topos of the border in, for example, the critical concepts of border epistemology,[35] critical border thinking,[36] border rhetorics,[37] and mestiza rhetorics.[38]

Whereas the local (non-European) tacitly serves as the dialectical negation to globalization, the local serves as the mere inversion of the universal. If location is written off as the source of hegemonic universalism and simultaneously it is posed as the source of legitimate resistance to hegemonic universalism, then location is what had always already served as the hinge "of the expropriation of the impropriety of the other."[39] There is no difference between the local and the global, in other words, for one is always the condition of possibility of the other—we get both simultaneously.[40]

Abraham Acosta marked this impasse in *Thresholds of Illiteracy: Theory, Latin America, and the Crisis of Resistance*, in which he reads the production of orality and literacy as a discourse through which all ethnocultural difference has been read in Latin America. In Latin American cultural discourse, and in critical discourse about Latin American writing, orality and literacy *together* represent an iteration of the presupposition of primordial Western/non-Western difference. In other words, while the figurations of non-Western difference have taken many different forms (orality, indigenismo, mestizaje, testimonio, etc.), cultural and political critique in the region has never *not* presupposed this foundational difference; signification in Latin America has never *not* been understood as either literate or oral, Western or non-Western, mestizo or European. This binary thus facilitates the formula for a theory of cultural politics: enlist the self-evident and culturally authentic semiosis of subalternized, non-Western groups as a counterhegemonic rhetoric of resistance to Western narratives of modernity.

Yet problems lie at the foundation of this reasoning. The problem that orality lays bare is nothing more than its marginalized and excluded position *within* the institutions of literacy and culture—orality does not, and can never, signify an untouched beyond literacy's conceptual gaze, for orality and literacy are defined by each other. They are not self-evident, objective categories but rhetorical categories that participate in inventing knowledge:

Orality and literacy must both be understood in their full biopolitical
capacity as their onto-epistemological figurations in culture and criticism
constitute the grounds of sovereignty and subalternity simultaneously.
Consequently orality's "liberation" from literacy's subordination is neither
itself the objective nor the problem; orality cannot serve as grounds upon
which to criticize or resist the West, for orality already lies at the heart of
the former. . . . The "problem" of orality and literacy in modern Latin
America is therefore no longer which of the two to privilege in cultural
criticism (orality *or* literacy) but rather to trace the limits of the inside-
outside relation itself (neither/nor) and to exploit the continuous threat
of indistinction upon which such dualities are always founded and which
are kept hidden from view.[41]

Acosta is right in arguing that a foundational antagonism, represented in the
relation of orality and literacy, serves as the hegemonic grid of intelligibility
through which all readings of difference have come to be understood in critical
discourse on Latin America. Literacy and orality (again, as the representation of
a wider West/non-West presupposition) are not merely descriptive categories
that describe cultures in their exteriority to each other but constitutive categories that are mutually dependent on each other for their meaning. These
categories *together*—not one or the other—form a system from which meaning is produced. Figurations of non-Western difference such as orality are not
simply self-evident, nonideological forms of representation but constitutive categories that are "only ever to be found within literacy itself. Orality is therefore
not a constitutive outside to literacy but is its founding and inner-most sovereign exclusion."[42] The figure of exceptional difference—whether it be Indigenous, hybrid, or hemispheric—can no longer *only* be read in opposition to the
West, for the positive content of what is considered "non-Western" can only bear
meaning differentially—as different from the West. The topos of exteriority
(locus of enunciation, mestizaje, orality) foregrounds an impasse internal to
politics: there is ultimately no outside of hegemony.

Displacement

In this chapter, I have been reading two seemingly opposed scholarly approaches
to rhetorical historiography that reach different conclusions through a shared

desire to extract a truth that is hidden and must be brought to light. Erin Graff
Zivin identifies this desire as "arche-logic": "an excavational mode of thought, a
cousin of a certain conservative philological tendency, that has as its foundation or
ground that which hides beneath it, an identifiable and revealable truth."[43] Like a
polygrapher, one who administers a polygraph to excavate the truth from a subject
by documenting psychophysiological changes during questioning, a poligrapher,
in Murphy's terms, documents how communities work toward their commonly
perceived goods to extract the truth of "what ought to be discovered for the good
of the community."[44] Decoloniality, on the other hand, seeks to excavate and liberate authentic rhetorical histories from a Eurocentricity that misrepresents them to
maintain asymmetrical relations of power. Together, these attitudes to rhetorical
historiography form a "perspective by incongruity" symptomatic of a commonplace will to know the truth of history that forecloses on the possibility of an
unknowable and yet to be written political future.[45] The stakes for rhetorical
thought are high here, for the possibility of an unconditional openness toward
anyone that would ground migrant hospitality would require one to make space in
thought for an incalculable and nonidentifiable alterity that is *unplaceable*.

This concept of unplaceability is important to my readings of disinvention,
from which I build on Victor Vitanza's cultivated mis/understanding of alterity
in historiographical discourse. Vitanza treats "history" as catachrestic, a meta-
phor without literal referent. In the context of a shared intellectual desire to
restitute alterity from the history of rhetoric, our problem is one of formalizing
alterity without error or misrepresentation, all the while knowing that representation is always an error or misrepresentation:

> Globally, what are the (in[ter]ventional) procedures? Let us count: For a
> traditionalist-realist, it would be Some Thing! (The object for the most
> part, is nonproblematic.) For a revisionist-modernist, it would be Noth-
> ing. (The object is but disappeared and thus highly problematic—which
> leads to the principle of negative-epistemology, which in turn simulates a
> nostalgia for and a return to "Some Thing.") For a postmodernist, how-
> ever, it would be Some More—which can be mis/understood as either
> the negative (the impossible, lack) producing excess or can be mis/under-
> stood as pure affirmation (desire) producing excess. . . . In both forms,
> however, excess—and this is the important point—produces an over-
> whelming and unaccountable resistance to and disruption of any and

every attempt by modernist-revisionists to seize the (nostalgic) fantasy of "Some Thing," that is, to turn fantasy into a new, but this time true, political reality. Excess, therefore, is a mis/state of perpetual demystification, perpetual paraethical in(ter)vention, or a constant rude (interruptive) reminder that "reality" is a fantasy construction, is always already an object of a preexisting gaze, or ideology, and that there is no single act (of acts) that will strip away this mystification, or false consciousness! so that we can get to the promised land![46]

Vitanza reads a semiotic gap that fails to register on dominant grids of intelligibility but also fails to be appropriated by them. This exorbitance challenges the assumption that a subject of difference ("Some Thing") exists out there and can be excavated to tell the truth. The subject of difference is the effect of a rhetorical displacement, or a rhetorical disinvention that operates as though it were an object of knowledge that supersedes the processes of representation and that therefore points to ontic political realities as they truly exist.

I'm not going to suggest that we relinquish a commitment to truth. At the same time, though, in this book I am drawn to investigate sites of speech that are issued from beyond commonplace and that provide access to different kinds of truths. How are we to conceptualize rhetoric beyond commonplace? Can existing rhetorical concepts lend descriptive power to the formation of enunciations without loci? If so, how would our ideas of rhetorical invention change? Would rhetoric itself become dis-placed, removed from its proper place, or is a supplementary dis-placement always constitutive of rhetoric?

To conceptualize rhetoric without commonplace, I want to work through an impasse immanent to commonplace itself: if no pure non-Western location exists from which to assess Western imperialism from beyond its influence, then where does this leave the university as a Western civic institution, as one such location where the task of thinking beyond what counts as reasonable (according to the reason of the strongest) might still take place? Certainly, this thought *takes place* at public universities, in the transitive sense, but what does thought take? Land, for one thing. In the United States, public universities invent arguments that justify their ongoing occupation of Native lands. For example, public universities, a locus from which I write, say that they serve the people of the communities in which they are located, while the definition of community in such a commonplace rarely seems to include Native peoples. Or another example: epistemological decolonization might take place if one were to stop thinking from the locus of the West and instead think from non-Western topoi. And still, there is also a dimension of semiological exorbitance immanent to decolonial commonplacing, of something exorbitant immanent in appeals to decolonization issued from a locus of enunciation in a Western public university. Although decoloniality produces a topical theorizing of rhetoric, it never-theless also *requires* a nontopical, nonsubjective dimension, for if it were to be successful in decolonizing land, it would displace its own grounding as com-monplace in the process. Decoloniality, as a resource for inventing arguments, invents the necessity of its own displacement as a side effect.

Additionally, the critique of universalism in decolonial rhetoric is premised on the idea that universalism is a uniquely European phenomenon, emerging from a specific moment of economic expansion into the Americas. From this premise, universalism becomes synonymous with Eurocentrism and the legacy of colonial oppression. But as Charles Hatfield points out, "Universalism is nei-ther an ideology, nor a faith, nor an epistemology. It is intrinsic to beliefs, and it is thus present in every belief and in every rationality."[47] Our problem is not one that concerns universalism—as though one can somehow disavow the univer-salism ascribed to the Western canon by finding alternatives and assuming that they do not operate on the basis of universalism. Rather, our problem concerns the assumed position that the topos of difference is both naturally occurring and *inherently* resistant to the dominant commonplaces of coloniality. If the topos of difference produces mis/understanding, then we must also consider the possibility that the subjectivity associated with difference is also subject to mis/understanding. What we are dealing with is not a problem of a certain kind of subjectivity (that is, the wrong understanding of the subject) but instead a problem inhabiting the category of subjectivity itself. The possibility for a cri-tique of hegemony in rhetorical theory depends on the degree to which chal-lenges to dominant forms of reason do such work regardless of subject position. I pursue this by building on the category of subalternity. A critique of Western imperialism or the possibility for a critique of dominant historical narratives of progress and modernization can no longer find grounding in an alternative loca-tion as the truth of the subject for, as Gareth Williams contends, neither of these "allows for any counter truth or negation other than that of another loca-tion that one can only recuperate and articulate over and against that of the first location. The dialectics of location only produces more of itself."[48] Rhetorical theory might come to grips with the idea that neither location nor subjectivity guarantees a radical rupture from Eurocentricity.

We have inherited a critical discourse in which the ethical option is said to be found in either one or the other but never not one of the two. To explore new avenues for critical thought in rhetorical theory, we might start by interrogating this postulate of difference (its reasoning and implications) as a partition of the sensible (the order of order), for the quality of this deadlock may lie in a disinvention that takes the form neither of West nor non-West but of a discontinuity that binds both to each other and exposes their sheer contingency (their lack of any natural grounding). I want to come to grips with the idea that the practice of identifying the proper place of rhetorical forms as West or non-West produces an impasse. Hegemony functions via its ability to signify clear distinctions of space (example/exception, interior/exterior) and time (original/copy, authentic/fake). It must articulate a sense of the whole social text in which every body is in its proper place. There can be no remainders, no excluded parts. Any notion of counterhegemony grounded in exteriority takes up a resistance to this hegemony through the terms and conditions of this very grid, ultimately replacing one form of hegemony with another, which suggests that the universalism ascribed to Western epistemology is not the problem. The problem rather seems to be the antagonism between hegemony and its own internal foreclosure.

My objective in this chapter has been to trace a disinvention within decolonial ideas of rhetorical invention to locate a space of disruption from *within* Western imperialism. The regionally local subaltern expressions that critics thought had provided a strategy of locating resistance to increasingly globalizing formations of capital (including the critical discourse of the university) have already been subsumed into the grammar of global capital itself. As Williams argues, neoliberal discourse in Latin America operates through a kind of neoprimitive accumulation, "an intensified drive within globalization to have subalternity be subaltern and to have it perform and speak its subalternity . . . in a regulated, market-driven, and whitewashed environment."[49] In other words, if the rhetoric of accounting for subjectivity and authentic cultural difference has become a fundamental operation of the reproduction of hegemony in Latin America, then not only does this indicate the exhaustion of the local as authentic but, more importantly, it foregrounds the role critical discourse plays in the production of the order of police. That is to say, the discourses of Latinamericanism, and of Latinidad for that matter, are already at the service of global capital, especially since one can hardly dispute the role of universities in the production of transnational power/knowledges.

If the objective of rhetorical theory all along has been to articulate the means by which thought can form an alliance with the university's other, I propose to do this by beginning from rhetorical disinvention, of which the failure to produce absolute knowledge can be productive of a form of inquiry other than what is determined by police.

3

Misidentification | Arizona HB 2281 and *No Te Entiendo*

We must desediment the dissimulation of a war.
—Nahum Dimitri Chandler, *X: The Problem of the Negro as a Problem for Thought*

On April 23, 2010, Governor Jan Brewer of Arizona signed the Support Our Law Enforcement and Safe Neighborhoods Act (Arizona Senate Bill 1070), which criminalized the unlawful entrance and presence of undocumented people in Arizona. Arizona SB 1070 was essentially a trespassing law that gave police the power to arrest, without a warrant, anyone suspected of being in the country unlawfully, in addition to requiring "aliens" to carry registration documents and outlawing transporting, and/or harboring "illegal immigrants."[1] What might have persuaded Brewer to sign the "toughest bill on illegal immigration"?[2] Brewer said, "There is no higher priority than protecting the citizens of Arizona. We cannot sacrifice our safety to the murderous greed of drug cartels. We cannot stand idly by as drop houses, kidnappings and violence compromise our quality of life. We cannot delay while the destruction happening south of our international border creeps its way north. . . . Today—with my unwavering signature on this legislation—Arizona strengthens its security WITHIN our borders."[3] Brewer is not the first to argue that migrants pose a threat to civic life, nor is she the first to mobilize this argument to wield the power of immigration law in the name of ethnoracial exclusion.[4] Nevertheless, Arizona SB 1070 crystallized Americans' perceived fears of the consequences of a growing Mexican American population: competition for jobs with Mexican laborers and the violence of Mexican drug cartels. SB 1070 also rendered visible the impunity of immigration policy, as it sought to secure civic life by reducing the number of migrants in Arizona. Fewer than twenty days after signing SB 1070 into law, on May 11, 2010, Brewer signed Arizona House Bill 2281, which prohibited Arizona public schools from teaching classes that were alleged to promote the overthrow of the U.S. government, promote racism and/or classism, or advocate ethnic solidarity rather than treat students as individuals and, additionally, prohibited courses supposedly designed for students of a specific ethnic group. And while the law does not explicitly name any ethnic or racial group as its target, critics have described it as a supplement to SB 1070 and conclude that these laws, together, confirm the targeted political exclusion of Mexicans and Mexican Americans in Arizona.[5]

I take as my entry point into this case a question of rhetorical invention. In Christa J. Olson and René Agustín de los Santos's introduction to "Expanding the Idea of América," a special issue of *Rhetoric Society Quarterly*, they "urge rhetoricians in the United States to recognize our own participation in the ongoing constitution of América and, in the process, re-think the Américan assumptions and implications infusing our scholarship."[6] As we ask after the rhetorical conditions through which América is rendered intelligible—through which someone or some people in the space of América are made subjects, are granted the right to be recognized as human—we ask after a regime of topoi through which intelligibility takes place altogether. I pursue in this chapter the question of the regulatory assumptions infusing ways of knowing and becoming known, by rereading the rhetorics of race in the context of SB 1070 and HB 2281.

As I argued in chapter 2, rhetoricians have dedicated more thought to studying rhetorics of cultural difference; however, a great deal of this work has turned on a discourse of mestizaje and transculturation as the grounds for rendering rhetorical production from underrepresented peoples intelligible.[7] Still, this question of rhetorical invention does not seem to encompass those who might not have a place in a mestizocentric regime of knowledge and intelligibility, those whose part in the borderlands is *atopic*, determined via their lack of part. And given that mestizaje has been practiced as a dominant discourse that serves to cement the colonial project of eradicating Indigeneity and Blackness, I believe it is time to move beyond a prevailing metaproject of looking to the U.S.-Mexico border as a topos of resistance to Eurocentric modernity, as the source of rhetorical invention from the assumed consciousness of a mestizo subject inaugurated by conditions of bordering. This metaproject is perhaps most visible in rhetorical studies of U.S.-Mexico border space, which critics continue to read through a mestizocentric grid of intelligibility to the degree that this space has become synonymous with this particular ethnic group.

This chapter begins with a reading of a rhetorical disinvention in an eighteenth-century casta painting titled *Las Castas*. The painting visualizes the formation of the mestizo subject in colonial Mexico through an active misunderstanding of Black and Native peoples. Black and Native people weren't excluded in the system of castes—they were included as topoi of unintelligibility. It's therefore not simple enough to imagine a society where they are reincluded, because they were never excluded to begin with. Rather, the problem was their inclusive exclusion from the very beginning in violent, colonial rhetorics of subject formation.[8] This chapter traces the way that Black and Indigenous figurations of inclusive exclusion begin to make their own infrapolitical reasoning and escape their violent framings in their states of being misunderstandable. I will argue that rhetoricians should try to misidentify with the legacy of mestizaje and perhaps some of the claims to decolonization that are grounded in mestizaje too.

I draw this reading forward into the second half of the chapter to investigate how the arrest of a Black woman in Arizona disinvents the genealogical mestizocentrism that grounds the fight for ethnic studies in the 2010s. I began to pursue this question in the summer of 2014, when Professor Ersula Ore of Arizona State University (ASU) was unjustly arrested for crossing a closed road on the ASU campus. Why weren't we talking about Dr. Ore's case, I wondered, with the ongoing police violence against Black men, women, and children *in conjunction with* the regime of ethnoracial violence directed toward the Mexican/Mexican American community in Arizona? How is it that Dr. Ore was a part of this political community who was nevertheless atopic within the rhetorical terrain of the dispute over SB 1070 and HB 2281? I argue that Dr. Ore's speech escapes the gaze of both mestizo and white onlookers on a street, and what escapes in her speech is a demand whose very exclusion enables the dispute over SB 1070 and HB 2281 to take shape.

Signatures of Disinvention

In a painting titled *Las Castas* (fig. 2) an anonymous artist arranges a taxonomy of racial castes, producing a visual representation of *la sistema de castas* in colonial Mexico. As critics have argued, *la sistema de castas* marked Spanish colonial efforts to produce and sustain social and political order when they themselves were a minority group in the eighteenth century.[9] *Las Castas* marks a visual

Fig. 2 | Anonymous, *Las Castas*, eighteenth century, oil on canvas. Museo Nacional del Virreinato, Tepotzotlán, Mexico.

production of this order, and it specifically visualizes the allocation of power along the genealogical account of miscegenation and racial identity. The painting categorizes racial mixture in the terms outlined in table 1. Given that the practices and forces of *la sistema de castas* are well documented, I will not recount the context surrounding *Las Castas*.[10] What is important to this book, however, is the infrastructural order of *la sistema de castas* rendered by *Las Castas*, an order that is organized along a set of premises that are fundamental to a discourse of race that continues to be produced in contemporary critical thought. *Las Castas*, in particular, renders the ideological core of *la sistema de castas*, which itself serves as the structural arrangement of the discourse of mestizaje.

Table 1   Racial Mixture in *Las Castas*

Español + India	(1) Español + India = Mestizo (1/2 India) (2) Mestizo + Española = Castizo (1/4 India) (3) Castizo + Española = Español (0/0 India)
Español + Black	(4) Español + Mora = Mulato (5) Mulato + Española = Morisco (6) Morisco + Española = Chino
Black + India	(7) Chino + India = Salta atrás (8) Salta atrás + Mulata = Lobo (9) Lobo + China = Gíbaro (10) Gíbaro + Mulata = Albarazado (11) Albarazado + Negra = Cambujo (12) Cambujo + India = Sambiaga (13) Sambiago + Loba = Calpamulato (14) Calpamulto + Cambuja = Tente en el aire (15) Tente en el aire + Mulata = No te entiendo (16) No te entiendo + India = Torna atrás

The painting generally narrates three clusters of mixture. The first three castes visualize the traditionally understood conception of hybridity in Latin America, the mixture between Spanish and Indian, or mestizaje. Castes four through six visualize the mixture between Spanish and Black, and finally, castes seven through sixteen visualize the mixture between Black and Indian. What should be emphasized here is the loophole in the logic of mestizaje concerning the role of whiteness. In the first cluster, the Spanish-Indian mixture, whiteness is produced in the third generation of mixture. The last two clusters of mixture, Spanish-Black and Black-Indian, never produce whiteness. One notices here that whiteness can be produced—inherited, rather—as long as Spaniards mix with Indians. But not Black. As soon as Blackness is introduced, it is impossible to return to whiteness. In addition, there is a gendered element to mestizaje confirming that it is a process of whitening that is hostile to and defined against white-Black mixture (*mullataje* is, instead, the name for that mixture). In the latter two forms of mixture in the first cluster, men of mixed-race identity are mixed with white women. And in the third generation, an "Español" is produced. However, in the second cluster, the very same gendered formula is presented (woman of color in the first form, white women in the latter two), and the result is "Chino." The meanings of the names of specific castes are subject to debate, though Marco Polo Hernández Cuevas argues that the word *chino*, which is often translated as the adjective "Chinese," instead refers to the racial caste born of mixed-race parents. Cuevas writes,

> "Chinos" are Afro-Mexican "chinos-cambujos," çambujos, or zambujos. "Chino," in New Spain archival records, generally, is a referent to people of African heritage whose lineage was perceived by the Spanish and other Europeans as "tainted" by African blood. Therefore, they were labeled "chino," a synonym for "pig" in the Murcia region of Spain; or "chino-cochino" (dirty pig). Although the animal connotation of "chino" has disappeared, the "dirty" lineage implied by the term has survived until present; curly hair in Mexico is "pelo chino." The general usage of the homonym "chino," meaning Chinese, emerged in nineteenth-century Manila, Philippines as a synonym of Sangley, the name given to Chinese merchants.[11]

Las Castas visualizes mestizaje's infrastructural organization: mestizaje is a process of whitening, a procedure of purification through directed mixture. Mestizaje appears felicitous because it is predicated on the production of Blackness as an unreadable part of the social text, as the group that cannot be purified and reformed into colonial society. This logic of inclusive exclusion of Blackness is the condition of possibility for mestizaje's articulation in the first place, and it is the exclusive textual form from which mestizo identity takes shape. Blackness appears, in Nahum Dimitri Chandler terms, as the figure of the X—the "figural figure that is no figure." Of the figure of the X, Chandler writes, "we can recall that X of the shuttling signature that remains of the unnamed and unnameable Negro or African American slaves."[12] In *Las Castas*, the *no te entiendo* marks this unnamed, unnameable figure that is no figure.

Derrida's reflection on the rhetoric of the frame in *The Truth in Painting* will help me unpack an emergent and exorbitant dimension of rhetoricity in mestizaje. Derrida reads Immanuel Kant's conceptualization of the universal value of beauty in the "Analytic of the Beautiful," noting that Kant defines the beautiful as the bounded, such that aesthetic judgment is not involved in anything beyond itself. A work of art is beautiful because it has boundaries, because it is enframed in its own domain. According to Kant, art is autonomous, and its *parergon*, its frame, grounds its autonomy as art. The frame of a painting, for example, allows one to read the difference between art and the wall it is hanging on beyond the painting's field of representation. The frame, neither inside the field of representation nor totally outside it, nevertheless separates interior from exterior. However, in establishing the rhetoric of the frame as the means to mark the proper site of aesthetic representation against its exterior apparatus of display, Kant encountered an aporia, for the frame is part of neither the art work (*ergon*) itself nor the wall but something altogether different. From the perspective of the wall, the frame is an interior component of a painting; from the perspective of the painting, the frame forms a component of the wall exterior to the painting's field of representation. The frame is therefore *parergon*, and there can be no absolute certainty as to whether the frame belongs to the interior or the exterior. The painting's field of representation becomes the domain of art only through its difference that is marked by the rhetorical frame.

Derrida notes that "frames (Einfassungen) of pictures or the drapery on statues, or the colonnades of palaces" are not simply peripheral to the works they decorate—they are supplementary: "What constitutes them as *parerga* is not simply their exteriority as a surplus, it is the internal structural link which rivets them to the lack in the interior of the *ergon*. And this lack would be constitutive of the very unity of the *ergon*. Without this lack, the *ergon* would have no need of a *parergon*. The *ergon*'s lack is the lack of a *parergon*, of the garment or the column which nevertheless remains exterior to it."[13] I read the frame as an infrapolitical signature of structure. At stake in the questioning of the frame, or in noting that the frame exists to produce the value of an object that is itself lacking any value unto itself, is the revelation that structure itself never assumes a disinterested, transcendent value. In other words, anytime one witnesses an instance of structure, one realizes that there is an excluded part from which structure assumes both shape and value. Any and every structure is therefore bound to that which belongs "outside" it. Still, and more radically, Derrida defines the *parergon* as parastructural—an element that cannot be thought within the conditions of the structure, given that the *parergon* discloses the aporetic site from which the structure is built. In referring to the "insistent atopics of the *parergon*," Derrida contends that the *parergon*'s paraplacement serves as a condition of both possibility and impossibility: "neither inside nor outside, neither above nor below, it disconcerts any opposition but does not remain indeterminate and it *gives rise* to the work."[14] The frame, therefore, is not simply out of place, incorrectly placed, or placeless. The frame is atopic.

From the atopia of *no te entiendo*, one can read a disinvention in *Las Castas*: in the production of *no te entiendo* as the parergon that produces mestizaje. *No te entiendo* is the atopic and constitutive core of mestizaje, for without it, mestizaje ceases to makes (common) sense as the reasonable and proprietary form of racial mixture. From this vantage, mestizaje is a subhegemonic reason of the strongest, for mestizaje is premised on the capacity to be understood and known as the grounding of the political. The stakes of mestizaje, then, are to produce the figure of *no te entiendo* as an atopia that enframes mestizo cultural discourse. Indeed, as the cultural anthropologist Claudio Esteva-Fabregat has argued, mestizaje should be understood as the expression of a precise ideological field (as opposed to a self-evident phenomenon) driven by teleological will to synthesize Spanish and Indigenous cultures and bodies. The lynchpin of this ideological field is *no te entiendo* given that the drive for recombination in mestizaje "emphasizes the exclusion of the African, at least as the key to an ideological dialectic."[15]

There is nothing radical about mestizaje, for the inclusive exclusion of the figure of *no te entiendo* is the primary condition of possibility for mestizaje to take place as the felicitous and politically resistant outcome of the process of hybridization. I'm suggesting that the commonplace of the mestizo as a figure of cultural or racial political resistance comes with unintended and uncontrollable semiological baggage. Rhetorical inventions grounded in the commonplace of mestizaje produce a constitutive exception on which they depend and which they efface: Blackness. As *Las Castas* makes clear, one sees a signature of anti-Blackness constituting the discourse of mestizaje, which is confirmed, in José Vasconcelos widely cited text, *La Raza Cósmica*.[16]

At both an aesthetic and rhetorical register, *Las Castas* produces at least three structures of race. (1) First, it outlines a racial formation, assigning caste to bodies and bodies to place on the basis of caste. This code assigns a value to the law and technique of exchange; it establishes the right and wrong arrangements of mixture. (2) As such, within this law of racial value and exchange, certain forms of mixture are allowed or prohibited. An *Español*, for example, mixes with an *India*, not a *Mora*. (3) At the threshold of these codes, between (1) explicit and (2) implicit laws, between the (1) arrangement of the social text and (2) the truth of the social text that becomes nomos, there is a form of exchange in which structure itself is mediated. Here, one reads the first condition of possibility for such an order—not simply that bodies themselves *can be structured* but, equally important, that the order of race emerges *only* in the process of exchange and mixture. In other words, if bodies can be ordered—grouped, distinguished, and then regrouped and redistinguished based on the selection of different criteria— then the grounds for *any* order become differential. The discourse of race perhaps cannot be said to exist within the bounded box of each caste but in the *parergon* that one reads as the supplementary work of a gutter bounding one caste from another. Indeed, one is never provided with a caste that holds value sufficiently unto itself, for even if *Español*, *India*, or *Mora* did exist prior to the text of the painting, its narration, here at least, remains an impossibility. One can read a bounded racial identity only at the register of a disinvention—in the presupposed but entirely unintended and emergent supplementary frame that can never be sufficient unto itself. I contend that it is possible, therefore, to read hybridity in precisely the opposite way that it is traditionally understood to operate: not as the impure result of pure, preexisting racial identities but, rather, as *the* primary rhetoricity producing ethnoracial subjectivities in the first place.

Arizona HB 2281

Shortly after Arizona HB 2281 became law, then–Arizona Superintendent of Public Instruction Tom Horne released a public document calling on Tucson Unified School District to eliminate its Mexican American Studies courses, which he found in violation of HB 2281. Horne offered his rationale in the following terms:

> It is fundamentally wrong to divide students up according to their racial group, and teach them separately. In the summer of 1963, having recently graduated from high school, I participated in the civil rights march on Washington, in which Martin Luther King stated that he wanted his

children to be judged by the content of their character rather than the color of their skin. . . . I believe it is a principle adopted by the legislature and the governor when this statute was passed. The Ethnic Studies courses in the Tucson Unified School District teach the opposite of this principle.[17]

In Horne's reasoning, the role of the state is to maintain a civic space free from ideological supplementarity, where citizens pursue education free from any ideological distortion of reality (of which he accuses ethnic studies). So how does Horne weaponize Dr. King's egalitarian rhetorical project against ethnic studies? Horne misidentifies with Dr. King's message, but there is something more at work here. Horne reframes ethnic studies within the ethos of Jim Crow, insisting on policy change as a nonideological solution. Students are entitled to be treated fairly, he reasons, not on the basis of their skin color (i.e., not on ideological grounds of race). Ethnic studies reintroduce race back into civic space, he reasons, instituting an ideological, and therefore fundamentally unethical, form of subjectification. Horne's misidentification with Dr. King goes beyond mere appropriation: Horne doesn't simply cherry-pick one part of Dr. King's message, but rather, he reinvents Dr. King's argument by assigning a new signified to the sign "equality." Horne deploys Dr. King's commonplace ("I have a dream that my four little children will one day live in a nation where they will not be judged by the color of their skin, but by the content of their character") to signify the dream of a color-blind civic space. It would be pointless to engage Horne on the grounds that he misappropriates Dr. King, for Horne is taking Dr. King at his word and reassigning meaning to the signs themselves.

Horne reinvents Dr. King to patch the rupture to civic space that Dr. King's speech introduced in the first place. In formal terms, Dr. King's "I Have a Dream" speech ruptured civic space because it reminded us of the fracture on which *every* political community in the United States is originally constituted: that there existed in the structure of the nation-state a "part of no-part": a set of Black humans who were included within the public space of the state via their exclusion from it and could therefore claim no proper place within it.[18] Dr. King reminds us, in other words, that there is ideology when there is said to be none—he reminds us that the civic space is neither self-evident nor ideologically neutral but one that naturalizes and maintains itself on the basis of a foundational logic of inclusive exclusion of Black humans. Horne's statement turns on inventing this rupture to the point that it *could* appear without revealing the fractures in the grounds of civic space. From this invention, Horne wages the claim that it is ethnic studies that introduce an ideological supplement to the civic space that he assumes to be ideologically neutral.

Horne's statement enlists race not only to authorize an already entrenched, and unacknowledged, racial hierarchy but to enlist the form through which this hierarchy is established ("it is not me but they who are the real racists"). Horne's argument, in other words, ultimately operates by attempting to conceal and ban this ungovernable ideological excess. The argument presupposes a political field where everyone has their part and no supplement to the civic space exists except for that which is unequally asserted after that fact (race). Horne's statement wages an argument against ideology *in general* (as a proposal to eliminate rhetoric from politics). Nevertheless, there is a moment of semiological excess in his argument that articulates precisely the opposite of what Horne perhaps intended: that the sovereignty of the nation-state is in fact just as invented as ethnic studies.

When critics have discussed this case, they have tended to critique the role the state played in instituting an anti–Mexican American civic space. I want to show how these critiques turn on the very same rhetorical form Horne uses (the accusation of ideological supplementation from a nonideological locus). Take note, for instance, of Anna Ochoa O'Leary, Andrea Romero, Nolan Cabrera, and Michelle Rascón's attempt to reinvent the inequality the bill attributed to ethnic studies. They argue, in diametric opposition to the legislation, that "legislative policies such as HB 2281—not the [Mexican American Studies] courses—create racial division and feelings of resentment in Arizona. HB 2281 is ideologically motivated legislation designed to keep other people of color from recognizing their commonalities, developing coalitions, and creating stronger democracy in Arizona."[19] It is the state, in other words, that institutes racial inequality.

In a similar fashion, Tony Diaz, an activist, community college instructor, and self-described *Librotraficante*, organized a caravan to smuggle books banned by HB 2281 from Houston back into Tucson. The caravan made stops for teach-ins, public readings, and protests along the way, and when the caravan arrived in Tucson, volunteers distributed the books from a taco truck. Diaz writes, "It is obvious Arizona legislators were trying to prevent other Latinos from becoming empowered with knowledge when they passed House Bill 2281 that prohibits courses which authorities deemed 'promote the overthrow of the United States government.' That's what they believe books about our culture will do: Overthrow the government. . . . Our aim is to change the system so that it better reflects the students in classrooms around the country. The Tucson Unified School District deemed only one course that dangerous: Mexican-American Studies."[20] The dispute here is not simply that of determining who is more racist. Instead, the more essential dispute concerns the fight over what the sign "equality" is supposed to signify. Whereas Horne claims that ethnic studies turns this signifier into an ideological and racist form of identification, Diaz claims that the state charges ethnic studies with an ideological and racist form of identification. Additionally, as Diaz conflates Latinidad with Mexican American subjectivity, his conclusion of "[changing] the system so as to better reflect the students in classrooms around the country" reads purely ideological, considering that his attempt at reinstituting institutional representation on the grounds of cultural heterogeneity is predicated on a different kind of truth (the truth of ethnic identity).

This rhetorical form is not limited to scholarly or activist rhetorics. It grounds the Modern Language Association's (MLA's) reflection on this dispute as well. The MLA's Executive Council released a document following its February 2012 meeting, titled "Statement on Tucson Mexican American Studies Program," which outlines its position statement against HB 2281 and offers the following conclusion:

> Although Arizona HB 2281 was ostensibly passed to ensure that students would be taught as individuals, we see the law as part of an attack on Mexican American citizens and cultures—including, but not limited to, undocumented immigrants. . . . Furthermore, we contend that the law has been discriminatory in effect, insofar as the superintendent's ruling, the judge's decision, and the school board president's order applied it to target and shut down only Mexican American studies programs. We note that programs in Native American and African American studies seem not to have triggered fears and anxieties among the supporters and enforcers of HB 2281.[21]

The MLA's statement renders an assumption that is shared by both parties of this dispute and that, additionally, reveals the mutually exclusive grounding on which this dispute turns. The attribution of the assault on ethnic studies to the Mexican American community, despite its centrality in Horne's campaign, amounts to a conflation of ethnic studies with Mexican American subjectivity and, in turn, the conflation of ethnoracial difference *itself* with Mexican Americanness. In Horne's argument, Blackness exists only as a whitewashed memory serving to qualify his fantasy of racial equality in a public sphere devoid of both race and ideology. Horne, of course, never acknowledges the existence of Black students living in Tucson and attending local schools, nor does he explain how his proposed ethnic studies ban might produce educational equality for Black students precisely because Black students don't exist in the Tucson constituted by his argument. In Horne's argument, ethnic studies signify Mexican American studies. In similar fashion, as the MLA "[sees] the law as part of an attack on Mexican American citizens and cultures," the MLA is only able to perceive a politics of the borderlands within the same mestizocentric regime of recognition. Whereas Horne, in the name of equality, frames the category of race as ideological residue to claim that ethnic studies are operating ideologically, the MLA, in the name of reality, frames the state's attack on a specific ethnoracial group to claim that it is the state acting ideologically. Whereas for Horne equality has nothing to do with ethnic identity, for the critics of HB 2281 ethnic identity is the grounds of equality.

The dispute over Arizona HB 2281 and SB 1070 turns on a rhetorical situation in which two mutually exclusive positions stake a claim on truth by claiming to eliminate the rhetorical fluff that is accused of producing political inequality. This dispute becomes an impasse, which is what happens when the dispute is reduced to the false choice of determining the "proper place" of the excess part of civic space: either you support freedom and democracy (reject ethnic studies, support immigration reform) or you support freedom and democracy (reject immigration reform, support ethnic studies). But there is more to any political process than can be represented by the terms governing it. My reading of this dispute is that, similar to the atopia structuring mestizo intelligibility in *Las Castas*, there is an ungovernable and excessive locus of disinvention, whose unintelligibility is a necessary condition for the dispute to take place at all. My goal in the remaining pages of this chapter is both reductive and expansive: to cast an impression of who cannot be heard from the terms governing this dispute (and perhaps what cannot be figured at all) and, additionally, to expose this atopia and its semiological dimension that precedes all rhetorical invention.

Misidentification

The political terrain of HB 2281 has, so far, turned on a normative, mestizocentric grid of intelligibility. If we revisit the political terrain of HB 2281 from the perspective of Dr. Ore's arrest we can begin to see how mestizocentric rhetorics of HB 2281 police the imagining of political community at the U.S.-Mexico border. We might better understand that the stakes of HB 2281 concern more than just the parties understood to have a stake in it and, instead, prepare for a political coalition among everyone who would be affected by the legislation. My argument is that we might better account for the rhetorical dynamics and the stakes of fallout from HB 2281 by witnessing the story of someone whose speech teaches to us that the work of intervention in power/knowledge is ongoing. But the issue I raise is not as simple as "listening" to the subaltern; instead, I ask after a modality of speech generated in the gap between those in a dispute and those whose exclusion from it makes the dispute perceptible.

Dr. Ore crossed College Avenue on the ASU campus (which was closed to traffic at the time) on May 20, 2014, when the ASU police officer Stewart Ferrin stopped her, requested to see her driver's license, and warned her that she would be arrested if she did not comply. She refused, and Ferrin placed her under arrest. Ferrin alleged that she resisted, and she was charged with aggravated assault and resisting arrest. The police report concedes that Dr. Ore was right to avoid the sidewalk construction. Nevertheless, Ferrin indicated that he initiated contact with her because she was in violation of ARS 13-2901, which describes the violation in terms of either "recklessly [interfering] with the passage of any highway or public thoroughfare by creating an unreasonable inconvenience or hazard" or intentionally activating a pedestrian crosswalk signal without the intent to cross. Ferrin arrested Dr. Ore for "failing to provide ID." No statute in the city of Tempe, Maricopa County, or Arizona state code requires one to produce a driver's license when requested by a police officer. A statute in the state code does exist (ARS 13-2412, "Refusing to provide truthful name when lawfully detained"), but it says only that a person must truthfully provide their full name when prompted by a police officer and, even then, only after they have been lawfully detained. The statute mentions nothing about producing a state-issued identification card or driver's license.[22]

The case prompts me to revisit some of my most intimate assumptions about rhetorical invention and politics. I read a trace of this thought in Dr. Ore's own reflection of her arrest in her article "They Call Me Dr. Ore," where she locates her street crossing not within, and on one side, of the police/Black U.S.-American antagonism but in the terrain of another, differently intelligible act of crossing where spaces of political community are indexed by racial intelligibility. Dr. Ore recounts her move south, from the northeastern United States to take a job in Arizona:

> When I announced that I'd be taking the job at Arizona State, friends and colleagues joked about my need to be careful. "Do you have your papers?" was a question I was regularly teased about, given that Arizona had just passed Senate Bill 1070, a bill that rendered non-whiteness—specifically, brownness—as "reasonable suspicion" to stop, interrogate, and detain drivers. I asserted that I'd be fine. "I pass the brown paper bag test," I joked. SB 1070 follows suit with Stop and Frisk legislation, except it specifically targets brown bodies, as these are the bodies considered within the broader context of Arizona border politics as "bodies out of place." While I knew Arizona was dangerous, I nonetheless considered myself "safe." In my mind I was less likely to be policed because unlike the Mason–Dixon of home, Arizona's border politics demanded brown bodies, not Black ones. Or so I thought.[23]

"I'd be fine," Dr. Ore jokes, reversing the logic of the brown paper bag test and indexing differential grids of racial intelligibility based on the location of their political borders: Blackness along the Mason–Dixon, Brownness along the U.S.-Mexico border. In the Northeast, border police demand Black bodies; in the Southwest, border police demand Brown bodies. Dr. Ore writes that she took this as a measure of her belonging and safety. She writes of the danger that a Black woman assumes as an out-of-place body in Arizona, though, in her words, she believed until after her arrest that the politics of U.S.-Mexico border space had nothing to do with her body. To whom exactly is she comparing herself, and what are the terms and conditions of this comparison? If she fails the brown paper bag test (her Blackness doesn't register as different enough) and the whiteness test, how then does she register on this white/Brown grid of intelligibility?

Dr. Ore's arrest challenges this normative racial grid of intelligibility, which produces Brown skin as evidence of unlawful presence in the United States and white skin as evidence of citizenship, as the dominant mode of perception along the U.S.-Mexico border, and which is produced most recently by the antagonism surrounding HB 2281 and other forms of legislation supposedly targeting specific subjects of undocumented migration (Brownness). Ultimately, it is this grid of racial intelligibility that produces civic identity and belonging in this situation, which prompts me to reconsider a foundational assumption about undocumented immigration: that immigration legislation targets, very specifically, a certain Brown body type. Certainly it does. However, that isn't the whole story either.

I read the HB 2281 ethnic studies antagonism with Dr. Ore's arrest, for they are differential parts of the same discourse of undocumented immigration in Arizona. I read these cases together in the precise sense that Jacques Rancière defines politics, which deals with how bodies fit, materially and discursively, within a given space. How bodies fit is determined by a rhetorical process of perception, by how we are trained to perceive the distribution of bodies in a common landscape. Politics is the name reserved for whatever disrupts the normative relation between bodies and where they're supposed to be. Politics can be understood as a rupture in any regime of recognition that would designate a proper place for anybody. And it is in this sense, I claim, that a rhetorical disinvention opens a clearing of racial politics from the negative affirmation of an alterity that cannot produce identification within any mestizo grid of intelligibility.

Dr. Ore appears in a dispute between grids of intelligibility—one mestizo and one produced and governed by the legal force of SB 1070 and HB 2281—a part that remains exorbitant and misidentifiable to both. Dr. Ore's case describes as a kind of misidentification: she is a subject who remains excessive to the formal topoi determining political belonging in the antagonism over ethnic studies. As Dr. Ore herself notes in her autobiographical account of the event, she cannot be categorized within the terms defining political belonging in this rhetorical situation, for "Arizona's border politics demanded brown bodies, not Black ones." And from the vantage of the dispute, she appears to reside outside of identification, of who can be identified, even as she remains subject to the demand for identification (in Officer Ferrin's hailing), given that there is no formal principle that determines whether her identity is intelligible or not.

Dr. Ore writes that the grid of racial intelligibility that she once saw as both self-evident and external to her body was in fact always already the way to understand her part in the political community of the borderlands: as the *misidentified* supplement from which political belonging takes shape *regardless* of her location. Perhaps this moment demonstrates that the terms by which Dr. Ore thought she was safely identifiable (that she passed the brown paper bag test) instead confirms that she was already reading herself from within the terms and conditions of this grid of racial intelligibility. Is it possible, then, that this moment in her account confirms that it is Dr. Ore's Blackness (as opposed to Brownness) that is the site of a misfire in power/knowledge from which to truly understand who belongs and who doesn't belong in the space of the U.S.-Mexico border? As she notes, in the Arizona context, what initially appears as a field of intelligibility producing Brown skin as the evidence of "illegal immigration," or the criminal threat of Brown bodies, instead reveals itself to produce *all* bodies of color as out of place. We can deduce that the same logic of exclusion drives the Mason–Dixon line.

Dr. Ore's account details a disinvention from which to think about speech and community in the U.S.-Mexico borderlands otherwise than their understanding in mestizocentricity:

> Stereotyped as hot-tempered, angry, and too smart for their own good, Black women like me get spread across cars in the dead of night as a sea of white onlookers picnic at a pub feet away and watch.
>
> Me: "I'm not invisible! I'm not invisible! Don't stand idly by and let this happen! I'm not invisible. I know you see me!"
>
> I don't shout "HELP!" because I know that assistance from others is not an option for Black women in the street, particularly when those women are tussling with white men in blue uniforms. I shout that I'm not invisible several times but no one moves except to stuff their mouths and drink their drinks as Black women like me get choke-holded and spun to the ground. My dress goes up when I hit the ground; the other officer knees me in my back as Ferrin partially dislocates my right shoulder to handcuff me. I scream because I know no one can see me on the ground. I scream because I've been taken down. I scream because I have no other means of expelling my rage and awareness that it will be my body along with Trayvon's and Michael's that will conclude the manuscript. I must be the one to get away if I want to live to speak another day. And so, rather than continue to fight back, I scream.[24]

Dr. Ore's shout demands her personhood beyond any predicate of intelligibility. It is a demand for personhood despite belonging and beyond what the state of Arizona deems as reasonable. In her momentary unbelonging—being included in the law's terrain (being made into a subject who violated a law, while remaining outside its protection from unfettered police violence)—the civic premise of representation based on recognition is pushed into crisis. If intelligibility is the condition required for affirming humanity, then from the perspective of mestizocentrism (representation based on numbers of a population), we would not be able to read Dr. Ore's shout as speech and, in turn, would not be able to affirm her personhood. If the fight over ethnic studies turns on instituting political representation from the grounds of intelligibility, then Dr. Ore's speech reveals that to be an impossible project, for those who have no part in this antagonism can *never* take part.

Dr. Ore does not ask for help because she says that intelligibility (a precondition for help) is not available to her. White onlookers drinking their beer and eating their food do not perceive her shout for help as speech. I believe this is important because the critical impulse might be to register her intelligibility as a way to affirm her humanity. I think it has to be the other way around. When she shouts, "Don't stand idly by and let this happen! I'm not invisible. I know you see me!" she issues an unreasonable demand—a demand that is itself absolutely reasonable but imperceivable (atopic) from the perspective of Arizona's normative grid of cultural intelligibility. Dr. Ore issues her demand *despite* the fact that she cannot be understood in that moment—despite any reasoning, hegemonic or not—and in this sense, exceeds the rhetorical ecology determining her (lack of) intelligibility in the civic space of Arizona. Something about her is intelligible *despite* the regimes of recognition determining her intelligibility. There is a different invention of her humanity—a disinvention in the form of an unreasonable demand—emerging only from her distance from intelligibility and irreducible to the normative rhetorics of race circulating in the rhetorical situation of HB 2281, that draws into relief the absolute limits of intelligibility. We are reminded that there exists another possibility for community, for being-in-common, in the U.S.-Mexico borderlands that cannot be reduced to the incessant and conservative demand for recognition. From this unreasonable demand, we catch a glimpse of another politics that itself appears unreasonable, beyond a translatable ideological claim: a weak force, by the other to come, a force incompatible with the force of the reason of the strongest or the teleology of an institutionalized practical reasoning.

It is only from the perspective of Dr. Ore's speech, a rhetoric issued from without commonplace, a speech beyond any predicates of belonging under Arizona's racial grid of intelligibility, that one can perceive the absolute limit of what speaking means and how it functions in this situation. I read Dr. Ore's shout as both the account of her obscured speech on which rhetorical invention in this antagonism is made possible *and* the speech of an alterity that cannot be apprehended within a mestizo or Anglo grid of intelligibility in Arizona. Dr. Ore's shout does not provide an account of any correct, right, or proper form of speech; however, it does reveal the absolute limits of what counts *as speech* in this situation and, in turn, the absolute limits of mestizocentric articulations of politics. Dr. Ore's speech implies an altogether different rhetorical form and pushes this rhetorical situation's representative function to its limit: it demonstrates the possibility of a mode of equality otherwise than what currently exists in Arizona, as "simply the equality of anyone at all with anyone else: in other words, in the final analysis, the absence of *arkhê*, the sheer contingency of any social order."[25]

We cannot assume that everyone has a shared capacity for speech (logos). This is simply because the capacity for speech is not biological—it is discursive. As Rancière writes, "Traditionally, it had been enough not to hear what came out of the mouths of the majority of human beings—slaves, women, workers, colonized peoples, etc.—as language, and instead to hear only cries of hunger, rage, or hysteria, in order to deny them the quality of being political animals."[26] People are denied their humanity when they are denied the capacity for speech—by being perceived as lacking the shared capacity of speech (logos). And this is why it's not enough to build knowledge on the assumption that one can hear the subaltern speak, for it isn't about a body's capacity to make sound but about how we perceive (or don't) a body's sounds as speech. And given that there are bodies whose sounds are not intelligible as speech (logos) but use intelligible language nevertheless, we run the risk of making this very same mistake when we assume that we hear the subaltern speak.

Dr. Ore's shout cannot be heard as a demand for identification, for as she notes, it would be impossible for white onlookers to perceive it as such. Does this mean that all white and Brown readers are unable to perceive Dr. Ore's demand? I'm not sure the question is mine to decide. But in any case, must the rhetoric of her demand—or the rhetoric of *any demand at all*—always be deliberative? A deliberative response will have been impossible. And yet, in Dr. Ore's demand, a disinvention emerges, with the effect that one can begin to misidentify with normative, mestizocentric demands for recognition as the grounds of politics.

4

Misunderstanding | Family Separations and the Lost Children

Numbers and maps tell horror stories, but the stories of deepest horror are perhaps those for which there are no numbers, no maps, no possible accountability, no words ever written or spoken. And perhaps the only way to grant any justice—were that even possible—is by hearing and recording those stories over and over again so that they come back, always, to haunt and shame us.
—Valeria Luiselli, *Tell Me How It Ends: An Essay in Forty Questions*

On April 6, 2018, United States Attorney General Jeff Sessions issued a zero-tolerance policy for offenses under 8 U.S.C. § 1325(a), which prohibits improper entry and attempted improper entry into the United States by any person who is not a U.S. citizen.[1] Zero tolerance directed U.S. Attorney's offices at the U.S.-Mexico border "to adopt a policy to prosecute all Department of Homeland Security referrals of section 8 U.S.C. § 1325(a) violations, to the extent practicable."[2] The fallout from the zero-tolerance policy was particularly destructive for migrant families and children crossing the U.S.-Mexico border. According to Border Patrol officials, before April 2018, "individuals who were to be referred for prosecution were generally processed by Border Patrol as single adults whether or not they were apprehended with their minor children."[3] Sessions's zero-tolerance policy marked a shift away from the Department of Homeland Security's "catch and release" practices, in which the Department of Homeland Security detained and deported families together or released families together into the community with a Notice to Appear—a document instructing a person to appear in immigration court for removal proceedings.

The zero-tolerance policy was designed to deter migrants from crossing the U.S.-Mexico border under the threat of family separation.[4] Whereas immigration officials had mostly avoided separating families by not referring "family unit adults" (adults entering the United States improperly with children) for prosecution, the zero-tolerance policy intensified the rate of family separations and child incarceration.[5] In March 2017, the El Paso Sector of the Border Patrol implemented a pilot program (The El Paso Initiative) for the zero-tolerance policy and suspended its "family unit policy," under which the Border Patrol did not refer family unit adults in violation of section 8 U.S.C. § 1325(a) for prosecution if it would cause parents to be separated from their children. In July 2017, a Border Patrol agent emailed Jim Tierney, acting U.S. Attorney for the District of New Mexico, suggesting that the District of New Mexico do the same, given the anticipated effects of family separation: "Although it is always a difficult decision to separate these families, it is the hope that this separation will act as a deterrent to parents bringing their children into the harsh circumstances that are present when trying to enter the United States illegally. . . . It is expected that once immigrants become aware that there is a higher probability of being prosecuted and separated if apprehended in Texas, the traffic will move to the areas surrounding the New Mexico Stations."[6] Migrants are framed here as "traffic," dehumanized figures to be managed in a major transportation project for screening those who will be granted entry and those who will be forced to take a detour to dead ends in remote areas of hostile terrain. While "traffic" might denote the movement of pedestrians or passengers, context suggests that the semantic range of the sign "traffic" here is narrowed to a biopolitical production of migrant families as intelligible objects of threats to U.S.-American sovereignty. Politics, under this heading of trafficking, would be reduced to its instrumental form for calculating the correct number of migrants to grant entry and justifying the criteria for determining such an account.

But there will never be a correct number of migrants to grant entry, for every attempt to justify such an account will result in an injustice. The question of how many migrants to allow entry is flawed because its premise, that there is a correct amount *at all*, is flawed. The Colombian musician Shakira made this point in a 2020 op-ed for *Time* magazine, in which she questioned the zero-tolerance policy that forcibly separated fifty-five hundred migrant families and detained nearly twenty thousand migrant children in federal facilities in 2018.[7] As of October 2021, parents had yet to be found and reunited with 545 children—60 of whom were younger than five years old when separated.[8] Shakira wondered, "What rationale could justify separating children from their families, with no intention of ever reuniting them, when the U.S. has prided itself on being a beacon of hope for those who come from places where not even basic needs or safety are a guarantee?"[9] One might ask in response, Is there a rhetoric, a right set of words drawing from the right topoi, uttered at the opportune time and delivered in the best arrangement suited to the ideal audience, that could justify separating migrant children from their families? Shakira's question asserts a proposition: while there will be words to describe what happened to migrant children and their families under zero tolerance, there will not ever be words to justify what happened to them, for a justification of family separations is an impossibility. Shakira's proposition is not that there is a right way of speaking about family separations such that one might arrive at the reasoning for justifying the practice. Instead, she can only defer to the absolute limits of justifying family separation, for it is an "unspeakable tragedy taking place at America's southern border."[10] Topoi to justify family separations are both present and absent here. Even as Sessions drew from commonplaces of security and sovereignty to locate a "reason of the strongest" informing zero tolerance, there will never be topoi for justifying the policy. Forcibly separating migrant families is an act that is not simply unreasonable. It is unspeakable, not in the sense that family separations are unrepresentable but, instead, that *understanding* family separations is simply not possible. It will only ever be possible to misunderstand what happened to forcibly separated migrant families—to perceive family separation as impossible to tolerate.

Additionally, Shakira claims that "[this] is not about politics. There is simply no justification for the harm caused to these innocent children."[11] No rhetoricity can justify the disaster of family separations. No practical reasoning can be made from representations of the trauma of family separations beyond their violent instrumentalization as commonplaces of arguments in disputes over federal immigration policy. There's no justifying the United States' legacy of separating children from their families—at the border, on the auction block, at the boarding school, or in the internment camp, among other commonplaces of U.S.-American hegemony. Shakira's argument distances itself from a reduction of this violence toward instrumentalized political arguments: "this is not about politics" means "this is not about a dominant logic of history that passes as practical reasoning for governmentality." "This is not about politics" retreats from commonplace appeals to politics as a form of population or traffic control. And neither is "this is not about politics" an apolitical appeal to the archaeological truth of this event beyond any artifice of representation. Shakira does not appeal to a solution, a practical reasoning, in the form of a new metanarrative or normative commonplace. We are not asked to decide on any course of action right now. We are only prompted to misunderstand family separations and all appeals that would justify the practice. This is not about politics but about a rhetoricity anterior and posterior to a practice of politics as traffic patrol.

I argued in chapter 1 that deterrence produces a "terministic screen" that frames migrants as objects of political management whose intelligibility is limited to serving instrumentally as commonplaces of arguments in support of or opposition to immigration policy.[12] In similar fashion, public rhetorics of immigration have tended to circulate topoi of the violence of forced family separations to invent practical reasoning for more humane immigration policy. But as Karma R. Chávez and Hana Masri argue, "even when framed as a refugee or humanitarian crisis and therefore supposedly separate from economic migration, images of children, which traffic in rhetorics of vulnerability and innocence, easily pair with the pro-family, pro-child rhetoric of the immigration rights movement to, paradoxically, justify the nation's maintenance and fortification of its borders in ways that harm all migrants."[13] José Ángel Maldonado notes that there is an aseptic condition of possibility for rhetorical invention at play in even benevolent desires for immigration reform, for "family-separation politics rely on the coding of indigenous people as immigrants in order to uphold the fantasy of a white-only and English-only America."[14] Additionally, as Lisa Flores reminds us, "The invocation of outrage surrounding child and family separation relies upon and reinscribes whiteness and heteronormativity."[15]

In this chapter, I ask after the possibility of a rhetoricity of migrant hospitality beyond this aseptic instrumentalization of violence with a reflection on a photograph of Angie Valeria and Óscar Alberto Martínez Ramírez and Valeria Luiselli's testimonial *Tell Me How It Ends: An Essay in Forty Questions*. In these texts, I read a misunderstanding—neither a cultivated ignorance nor an instrumentalized knowing, but a will to misunderstand—of deterrence that emerges from an excessive rhetoricity that cannot be narrativized and that disinvents immigration reform as the grounds for migrant hospitality. Even if representations of the trauma of family separations cannot establish commonplaces for more ethical immigration policy, I read them as a site of crisis internal to the possibility of knowing, grounding a politics that Abraham Acosta describes as "a response informed by, inclusive of, and *in the non-name of All*," which "obtains now as a most critical and historical imperative: that regardless of population size or history in the area, *every* minority group has the right to assert the right to representation *anywhere*—even against the most traditional and predominant among them."[16]

In the Non-name of Valeria and Óscar Martínez

At a press briefing on June 26, 2019, a reporter asked then–United States President Donald Trump, "Does the photo of drowned immigrants cause you to rethink any of your policies?"[17] The reporter was referring to the photograph of Oscár Alberto Martínez Ramírez and his twenty-three-month-old daughter Angie Valeria, whose bodies were found on the shores of the Río Grande in Matamoros, Mexico, after they drowned attempting to cross the river into the United States. In the photograph, captured by Julia Le Duc and published in the Mexican newspaper *La Jornada*, Oscár and Valeria lie face down in shallow water at a riverbank, surrounded by reeds. Valeria is tucked into Oscár's shirt, her arm still coiled around her father's neck.[18] The reporter's question was deliberative in nature, asking after the possibility of a change of mind, a reasoning to be made upon receiving signs issued from "los que nunca llegarán."[19] The question holds open the possibility for metanoia that supposedly grounds the enterprise of rhetoric and stages the major presupposition of instrumental theories of rhetoric, which state that rhetoric amounts to a use of speech for political or practical ends.[20]

The Associated Press circulated the photograph, and it was published in venues like *The New York Times*, *The Washington Post*, *The Chicago Tribune*, and *The Guardian*. The photograph became a commonplace of tragedy for normative persuasive power on all sides of public arguments about U.S. immigration policy. For some, the image of Valeria and Óscar served as evidence of the violence and impunity of deterrence-era U.S. immigration policy, prompting epideictic arguments for better, more humane policies at the border. Debbie Weingarten, for example, wondered, "How many times must a child wash up on a shoreline or collapse in the desert before the very force of our collective grief and rage throws the Earth right off its axis—or at the very least, shatters the policies that support such suffering and death?"[21] Then–Democratic presidential candidate Julian Castro wrote on Twitter that "Oscar and Valeria Martinez [*sic*] died on these shores—desperately crossing the river as a last resort for asylum. They aren't the first to be killed by Trump's immigration agenda, and they won't be the last if we don't act soon."[22] And with an estimated sixteen to nineteen thousand migrants on metering lists in 2019, for others, the figure of *los que nunca llegarán* prompted reasoning against the policy of metering, which in 2019 authorized U.S. Customs and Border Protection to place an arbitrary daily limit on how many people seeking asylum in the U.S. would be granted entry.[23]

For others, the photograph reasserted the importance of immigration policies grounded in the force of law. Ari Fleischer, the former White House press
secretary under former president George W. Bush, suggested during a debate on
the June 26, 2019, edition of *Outnumbered* on Fox News that Valeria's and
Óscar's deaths were in fact Óscar's fault. When the Fox News contributor Jessica Tarlov reminded Fleischer that "seeking asylum is legal," Fleischer responded,
"Then go to a checkpoint. Don't swim across a river with a child that can't
swim. . . . There's legal ways into America." He continued, "Come to America
properly. There are checkpoints, there are places where people can go to have
their asylum cases adjudicated and heard. But when you try to come to America
illegally, you take so much risk onto your own shoulders."[24] In a similar fashion,
Ken Cuccinelli, then-director of the United States Citizenship and Immigration Services, was questioned by a reporter about the photo and its relation to
policy: Would the photo "[end] up being what represents the Trump administration's policies on the [U.S.-Mexico] border?"[25] Would the photo adequately
capture the truth of this event? Would it adequately signify the consequences of
immigration policy? For Cuccinelli, the photograph documented the reason for
the tragedy. Even for Cuccinelli, there is no meaning to be made from this image,
other than its instrumentalization toward accounting for the correct measure of
how to manage the community of the United States: "The reason we have trag-
edies like that on the border is because, those folks, that father didn't wait to go
through the asylum process in the legal fashion [and] so decided to cross the
river and not only died but his daughter died tragically as well."[26] Fleischer's and
Cuccinelli's epideictic responses to reporters' questions about the rhetorical
power of the image represent the nation-state's position on immigration policy:
migrants are responsible for their own deaths because they knowingly cross into
the United States without authorization.

Answering the reporter's question ("Does the photo of drowned immigrants
cause you to rethink any of your policies?"), Trump instrumentalized the photograph toward an appeal to better, more secure immigration policies that he
claimed his political opponents were preventing: "If we had the right laws that
the Democrats are not letting us have, those people, they wouldn't be coming
up, they wouldn't be trying." The short answer to the reporter's question was, of
course, *no*. The photo would not cause Trump to rethink his immigration policies: "We're building the wall." Trump continued with his trademark red-herring
logical fallacies: "You have these caravans, women are being raped, and one of
the terrible things: children are actually being brought into slavedom. If you

look at what's happening, the cartels and the coyotes, they're getting rich because the Democrats refuse to change the loopholes."[27] Trump's response to the reporter's question appears to fit the pattern of his speech on the border: scapegoat Democrats for impeding his efforts at securing sovereignty. Still, Trump appears to be upset not about children experiencing harm but rather that a paramilitary organization is generating surplus value from them.

As both a juridical and cultural form, deterrence has produced a grid of intelligibility that reduces Valeria's and Óscar's bodies to instrumentalized commonplaces of tragedy to be enlisted in public arguments for or against immigration policy, even as public debates turn on questions about what the photograph represents and if it should be shared at all. The nonprofit organization Refugee and Immigrant Center for Education and Legal Services (RAICES) described in a Facebook post a decision not to share the photograph, noting, "The media wants you to view them as just another tragedy, more #'s to rack up migrant deaths. They will show you the graphic image saying it will make people 'care' or 'move them into action.' We think otherwise." RAICES instead posted an image of Valeria and Óscar with Tania Vanessa Avalos. In the image, a cropped photograph of Óscar and Tania holding their daughter is set against a white background and a caption that reads, "stop dehumanizing them." RAICES's post asserts that despite whether the photograph of Valeria and Óscar has a rhetorical potential to move viewers into action, Valeria, Óscar, and Tania were a family who, like any other family, wanted the best for their child. Still, despite not sharing the photograph, RAICES's post ends with a claim that mobilizes the figures of Valeria and Óscar for an argument against deterrence immigration policy: "Restrictions like 'Remain in Mexico' and the 'Metering' policy which rejects asylum seekers who come to ports of entry asking for protection are what caused these deaths and the countless others that occur on the border every day. We can no longer stand by as this administration continues to build walls. It's time we build bridges into our society, so that ALL members are afforded their rights and treated with dignity. #BuildABridge."[28] I am not suggesting here that RAICES's post has neglected to account for the full humanity of Valeria and Óscar or that the post intentionally participates in the same form of dehumanization that deterrence produces. And yet, even in the choice *not* to publish the photograph under an apolitical auspice, RAICES's post cannot but instrumentalize the memory of Valeria and Óscar as a commonplace of tragedy for inventing an argument to oppose deterrence.

In a similar but different fashion as RAICES, *The New York Times* published the photograph under an overtly apoliticial claim. After *The New York Times* published the photograph in an article titled "Photo of Drowned Migrants Captures Pathos of Those Who Risk It All," editors explained the decision, suggesting that despite concerns that "it would give the appearance of The Times making a political statement," they were "confident that the image stood on its own, reflecting the perils migrants on the border face, not a position on the issue of immigration."[29] The title of the article narrativizes the capture of Valeria and Óscar in overlapping photographic and juridical forms. The deterrence-era immigration policies that steered Valeria and Óscar into the capture of the hostile terrain of the Río Grande now steer the discursive capture of Valeria and Óscar into an instrumentalized commonplace that, as Teju Cole puts it, "does not particularly challenge those who wield the power of life and death over others."[30] *The New York Times* claims that the photograph of Valeria and Óscar, enframed in the "apolitical" and aseptic whiteness of the newspaper's print and digital pages, represents "the tragic consequences that often go unseen in the loud and caustic debate over border policy."[31] To whom do these consequences go unseen if the dispute over policy is so loud and eristic? Possibly not federal officials who draft policy, given their anticipation of the deadly consequences of deterrence in the early 1990s. And probably not a public readership of *The New York Times*, which in 2015 published an image of Alyan Kurdi lying face down on a Turkish beach in an article titled "Image of Drowned Syrian, Aylan Kurdi, 3, Brings Migrant Crisis into Focus."[32] As *The New York Times* would have it, the point of journalism is to document (to capture) and present the truth, which stands on its own, free from a political position on immigration policy. But such an apolitical (anideological) position is an impossibility, for as Slavoj Žižek reminds us, "the minimum necessary structuring ingredient of every ideology is to distance itself from another ideology."[33]

Like the dispute over whether the photograph represents the consequences or success of deterrence, these two mutually exclusive positions on publishing the photograph—RAICES's political position not to publish and *The New York Times'* political position to publish—constitutes what Jacques Rancière calls a disagreement, a situation in which "contention over what speaking means constitutes the very rationality of the speech situation."[34] The difference between RAICES and *The New York Times'* positions on publishing the photograph can't be filled by introducing additional knowledge or more precise definitions of load-bearing concepts like politics. In fact, the organizations both depart from the same political grounds as an alibi for mutually exclusive publication decisions. There is no rhetoric available for reducing the difference between these positions precisely because the difference turns on both what the photograph represents and what publishing the photograph represents.

The reduction of representations of Valeria and Óscar to commonplaces of arguments in support of or opposition to immigration policy (and between publishing and not publishing the photograph in turn) is a false choice. Perhaps we should take *The New York Times* at its word and read the photograph in its moment of truth. The deaths of Valeria and Óscar are not a temporary, correctable bug in the system of deterrence that more humane policies of immigration can fix. Their deaths are a symptomatic excess that demystifies the hegemonic field of immigration as a question of better policy and draws out the complicity of the opposing false choices that constitute it. There is no better or humane immigration policy, for deterrence-era immigration policy is predicated on producing migrant deaths. The photograph cannot provide practical reasoning to public debates about immigration for, like the other photographs in the ever-increasing public archive of violent images of migrants suffering, it depicts an injustice so constitutive of American civic life in the twenty-first century as to be a banal and expected consequence of national security. Still, Valeria and Óscar, as undocumented migrants and subjects of the state immigration apparatus, are formally a part of the United States even as they are not citizens and can take no part in its civic community. As "a part of those who have no part," Valeria and Óscar lack a designation like citizenship or asylum that would qualify their part in the civic community.[35] Nevertheless, in Žižek's words, "they belong to the set of society without belonging to any of its subsets. As such their belonging is directly universal."[36]

Misunderstanding

In the introduction to the chapter, I read in Shakira's op-ed the traces of an infrapolitical rhetoricity beyond any instrumentalization of the trauma of family separations. Shakira appealed beyond a metaphysics of the subject to a *comunidad malentendido* that does not yet have subjection in common and does not require knowledge of the other as a necessary or sufficient condition for extending hospitality to them: "If there was ever a time to show greater compassion to the immigrants in our communities, it's right now."[37] It does not matter who the undocumented migrants are. Their individual subject positions are irrelevant to a rhetoricity of hospitality toward undocumented migrants—whoever they may be. Building on my reading of Shakira's op-ed with Valeria and Óscar's universal belonging, I read in Valeria Luiselli's testimonial nonfiction book *Tell Me How It Ends: An Essay in Forty Questions* a rhetorical disinvention that makes space for rhetoricity of undocumented migrant hospitality beyond a metaphysics of the subject and grounded in a will to misunderstand.

U.S. federal law defines "unaccompanied children" as minors with neither "lawful immigration status in the United States" nor a "parent or legal guardian in the United States [who] is available to provide care and physical custody."[38] In 2014, the Obama administration declared a humanitarian crisis after U.S. Customs and Border Protection apprehended 68,541 unaccompanied child migrants, according to a document euphemistically titled "Southwest Land Border Encounters." That number of unaccompanied children apprehended in Southwest land border encounters has risen dramatically in recent years, up to 137,275 in 2023.[39] Luiselli writes about her experience as an interpreter for these children in an immigration court during the summer of 2014 in her testimonial book *Tell Me How It Ends: An Essay in Forty Questions*. Luiselli was assigned to administer an intake questionnaire to the children in Spanish, translate their responses, and form them into narratives that ground their appeals for political asylum in the U.S. This process is known as "screening." There's a lot at stake in screening, as the children's defense against their deportation hinges on their responses and Luiselli's translations of them. The process is difficult, for Luiselli has to translate at least three registers of meaning. She must (1) translate the children's responses from Spanish to English; (2) translate an intentionally nebulous legal apparatus that is designed to be inaccessible so that she can prompt the children to tell the stories that are intelligible to the law as valid grounds for asylum; (3) translate the complexity of the children's lives into a coherent narrative form that interfaces neatly with the legal criteria for asylum. This third register of translation, however, will prove to be impossible. The first question, for example, directly addresses the charge of improper entry against the children: "Why did you come to the United States?" If their answers don't amount to what federal immigration law counts as reasonable for the right to asylum, they will be deported. "But," as Luiselli writes, "nothing is ever that simple. I hear words, spoken in the mouths of children, threaded in complex narratives. They are delivered with hesitance, sometimes distrust, always with fear. I have to transform them into written words, succinct sentences, and barren terms. The children's stories are always shuffled, stuttered, always shattered beyond the repair of a narrative order. The problem with trying to tell their story is that it has no beginning, no middle, and no end."[40]

Screening requires the children to constitute themselves as subjects before the law by narrating their migration. Their subjection before the law depends on their capacity to narrate themselves as subjects. The problem is that subjects not understood to be in possession of speech are required to speak themselves into the possession of speech. Their capacity to be documentable, which depends on their capacity for speech, serves as the grounds of their defense. And so, when the potential for documentability is compromised because of their speech, so is the children's possibility for subjection.

At first glance, it appears that Luiselli is referring to some objective, non-ideological, universal order of narrative that determines what counts as narrative. Narrative order, in this dispute, operates as a differend: "the case where the plaintiff is divested of the means to argue and becomes for that reason a victim."[41] These children become divested of the means to argue through the very injunction to speak what is often unspeakable. And what are the means to argue, exactly? The capacity for speech, which is not a biological concept but a discursive one. This is precisely why the problem here is not that the children lack the correct words or the proper experiences. Nor is it that the children lack enough words to say. Nor is the problem an insufficiency on Luiselli's part in translating their words from Spanish to English correctly, for that matter. The problem is that the children must navigate an impossible rhetorical terrain to make a claim for legal sanctuary. Their speech is irreducible to what the law counts as speech—to what can be counted at all—precisely because there is a lack of commonality itself in this situation.

Narrative order, here, operates as a sign designating very different signifieds to each of the parties. To the law, narrative order designates that which the children's stories lack: the logos (truth and reason *as* narrative order). And to the children, narrative order designates the state of exception in which federal immigration law is grounded: the simultaneous exclusion and inclusion of the lost children.[42] In this sense, "screening" is the name for the trace structure of the absolute limits of narrativizability (and, simultaneously, reasonability) in *Tell Me How It Ends* that draws into relief a hegemonic register of signification on which immigration law turns. Screening is not merely the process of documenting the lost children—it is also a mode for reading a rhetorical disinvention, a counterpart dimension of unreasonability in *any* source of rhetorical invention in this situation that traces this gap between orders of reason. In short, an irreducibly exorbitant and uncapturable trace of signification between narrativizability and meaning forecloses any possibility of logos, of truth or practical reason, for the lost children. Even if the children were to perfectly narrate their migration, their stories would narrate them as out-of-place, atopic subjects in the rhetorical domain of deterrence.

The stories of the lost children are not narrativizable and do not serve as commonplaces to organize beliefs and actions. I suggested in chapter 1 that we will probably never know how many migrants have died because of deterrence. I suggested that a better understanding of that crisis is unavailable, as it is unlikely that a complete story of the crisis would persuade the state to overturn an unjust immigration apparatus. Similarly, it is unlikely that a full accounting of the lost children's stories would lead the state to approve more petitions for asylum. There are no commonplaces from which to draw the right words to be issued at the right time, by the right speaker, to persuade those who are on the other side of the policy aisle to extend hospitality to the lost children. Their stories might never form a commonplace from which more ethical forms of immigration policy could be invented. Instead, the figure of the lost children might only ever haunt and lend disagreement to the available commonplaces, repeatedly exposing "the reason of the strongest" to its absolute limit. There is no argument to be waged as there is no storehouse from which to draw rhetorical energy. Or, perhaps their stories, "shattered beyond the repair of a narrative order," are storehouses of social energy in a different way than rhetoricians have understood the concept of topos.

If the lost children and their stories of migration to the U.S. are "shattered beyond the repair of a narrative order," atopic to the degree of "that which cannot be fitted into the categories of . . . our understanding and which therefore causes us to be suspicious of it," then, following Michele Kennerly, one might ask, How ought things be sorted if these unsayable narratives are amplified and circulated?[43] Moreover, in what ways do the disinventions of the lost children rewrite conventional topoi relevant to the ongoing crisis of migration and, more generally, to the politics of hospitality?

Something that cannot be narrativized escapes the screening process, cannot be made to serve what counts as practical reason in the given order of deterrence. There is a rhetorical disinvention here in a remainder of inscrutable rhetoricity escaping from within the narratives of the lost children. Luiselli writes,

"Telling stories doesn't solve anything, doesn't reassemble broken lives, . . . but perhaps it is a way of understanding the unthinkable."[44] Luiselli is referring here to the rigged bureaucratic legal structure of asylum that demands unnarrativizable stories from migrant children as the grounds of their claim to asylum. It is unthinkable that systematically incarcerating and deporting migrant children, from the perspective of deterrence, is entirely reasonable. At the same time, we might re-turn Luiselli's claim here and say that the disinventions of the lost children form a rhetorical disinvention that helps us to *unthink the understandable*.

The fragmented stories of the lost children don't solve anything and cannot serve as a site of social energy for arguments about migration. But this doesn't mean that rhetoric is failing. Instead, atopoi generate tactical misunderstanding as a resource for rendering unreasonable given articulations of power that might appear to us as natural and reasonable. Atopias can serve to help us generate misunderstanding when there is said to be reason, for example, wherever the mistreatment of *any* child is said to be reasonable. Atopias cannot be narrativized and, in turn, cannot found a reason capable of regaining power. In the condition of unspeakability, undocumented migrant atopias nonetheless deterritorialize that which counts as reasonable.

Ultimately, we might have to consider that despite the implicit appeal for a kind of practical reasoning registered in *Tell Me How It Ends*, what the stories of the lost children force us to see is a validation crisis in a will to know. The point is not to try to find more unnarrativizable moments as sites of translation. Nor is the point to make atopos a countertopos for a new political logic. I suggest instead that the point is to ask after the structural injunction to know and translate alterity into intelligible university discourse in the first place. Atopias don't provide positive knowledge. They might, however, assist us in negating the will to know that structures undocumented migrant hospitality.

How might scholarship in rhetorical studies look if it weren't structured by the will to know? How do we begin to practice a new nomos of community that accommodates those whose stories cannot be rendered within the technology of a narrative order? How do we hold something in common with someone without the predicate of knowing why they arrived? How are we to make community with those whose stories may never arrive? We might be able to pursue a different nomos of community—one where putting unaccompanied minors in prison would be unthinkable, where asking someone *why* they arrived would be unnecessary—if we suspend the will to know, to document and capture, as the predicate for undocumented migrant hospitality.

Will it have been possible to think a community grounded not in identification but in a misunderstanding of the metaphysics of the subject altogether and a preparation of a community suited for anyone at all that might pass through its doors? Will it have been possible to imagine a world where screening the lost children or instrumentalizing the photograph of Valeria and Óscar in service of policy debates is unthinkable?

5

Undocumenting | Stranger Politics in *Codex Espangliensis* and *Documentado/Undocumented*

If university discourse, as the neoliterary, neoregional, or neo-Latin Americanist, can no longer be "a model of the ideal society," it can still be "a place where the impossibility of such models can be thought."
—Alberto Moreiras, *The Exhaustion of Difference*

I open this chapter with a reading of Emma Pérez's concept of the decolonial imaginary, in which I read an ambivalence in her framing of the interstice of history as both exterior and interior to Eurocentricity. This ambivalence reflects the complex ways in which decolonial thought challenges Western logics of dominance while also requiring it. I don't think this ambivalence disqualifies decolonial thought, and I make no attempt to resolve its tension. Instead, I want to read this ambivalence as a resource for thought. I then read the decolonial imaginary next to Krista Ratcliffe's widely cited and important concept of rhetorical listening. Given rhetorical listening's reliance on Anzaldúa's *Borderlands/La Frontera*, a root text of theories of decoloniality, I read a cross-talk between fields that ultimately share the same ambivalent resource.

I then place my reading of these texts within a broader historiography of Latinamericanist thought. I argue that what is at stake with decoloniality is an ambivalence toward Eurocentricity, from which it distances itself. Drawing from Gareth Williams's reading of transculturation during the national-popular epoch in Latin America and Moreiras's critique of the intellectual desire to capture difference in order to release it into the global epistemic grid, I suggest that globalized capital and decoloniality share in a generalized form of flexible accumulation.

Ultimately, this chapter argues for the benefit of moving past decoloniality and toward what others have called a "posthegemonic" register of thought. To this end, I shift to a reading of two performance-art texts by Guillermo Gómez-Peña: *Codex Espangliensis: From Columbus to the Border Patrol* and *Documentado/Undocumented: Ars Shamánica Performática*. In Gómez-Peña's texts, I read signs of disinvention at work—ungovernable and exorbitant rhetorical inventions. As *Codex* narrates the discovery of the Americas in reverse (the discovery of the Iberian Peninsula), it allegorizes an undocumenting rhetoricity that both can and can't be documented, which can help us to see how the category of rhetorical invention always includes more than just the possible means for discovery.

The Decolonial Imaginary

I begin with a reading of the decolonial imaginary, a paradigm of critical thought that presupposes that political community, democratic space itself, can be read as a documentable, whole entity with no surplus parts. In Emma Pérez's widely cited book *The Decolonial Imaginary: Writing Chicanas into History*, she advances the concept of the decolonial imaginary as a method of reading the silenced part of colonial history—the silenced Chicana voices that have been relegated to interstices of history by Western modernity. *The Decolonial Imaginary* turns on the articulation of a succinct counterhegemonic subjectivity outside of hegemonic mediation. The stakes of *The Decolonial Imaginary*, then, are to develop a thinking of politics "without the dialectical promise of a teleological history."[1]

The Decolonial Imaginary maintains an ambivalent distance from the interstice that it reads to be both interior and at the same time exterior to Eurocentric power/knowledge. In other words, for *The Decolonial Imaginary*, the topos of the interstice marks both the structural incompletion of history from its interstitial exclusion and the structural completion of history through its interior. The wager here is that the interstice can be documented "without the dialectical promise of a teleological history," or that the interstice is the location of a nonhegemonic subject position *because* it is excluded from hegemonic mediation.[2]

The Decolonial Imaginary hinges on a reading of a gap that can be filled with historical substance while at the same time keeping the historical future open to the future perfect tense—to a politics that will have arrived (in decolonized fashion) through the interstices of that which was always within colonial history itself. In the introduction to *The Decolonial Imaginary*, Pérez writes, "Foucault's methodology is useful to historians because archaeology seeks to uncover discursive practices by unmasking them. It is self-reflexive in intent, and it is in that self-reflection where coloniality is exposed. Through his own self-reflection, Foucault was undoing European history. . . . He concluded in *The Order of Things*, 'man is an invention of recent date. And one perhaps nearing its end.' In essence, he claimed that European white man would no longer be central to history and its interpretations."[3] This passage establishes the first presupposition of the decolonial imaginary in detail. Pérez reads discourse as that which masks a subject. Analysis, therefore, amounts to the practice of unmasking. The stakes of this practice, according to Pérez, are such that we misinterpret the subaltern subject and that this subject can and should be unmasked.

Furthermore, *The Decolonial Imaginary* proceeds along a reading of postcoloniality, which does not designate a historical condition after the end of colonization but a historiographical condition whereby previously functional political distinctions (friend/enemy, colonizer/colonized, metropole/colony) have waned to the point of indistinction. Postcoloniality is therefore the name for what happens to political identities—to democracy itself—under the conditions of coloniality. Thus, it is only through the representation of an irreducible gap between previously functional political distinctions, through a not-quite-reformed colonial subject—the very ambivalent ideological kernel of coloniality itself—that a subaltern subject might be read by an intellectual:

> The desire for a reformed, recognizable Other, *as a subject of difference that is almost the same, but not quite.* Which is to say, that the discourse of mimicry is constructed around an *ambivalence*; in order to be effective, mimicry must continually produce its slippage, its excess, its difference. The authority of that mode of colonial discourse that I have called mimicry is therefore stricken by an indeterminacy: mimicry emerges as the representation of a difference that is itself a process of disavowal. Mimicry is, thus, the sign of a double articulation; a complex strategy of reform, regulation and discipline, which "appropriates" the Other as it visualizes power. Mimicry is also the sign of the inappropriate, however, a difference or recalcitrance which coheres the dominant strategic function of colonial power, intensifies surveillance, and poses an immanent threat to both "normalized" knowledges and disciplinary powers.[4]

The ambivalence of colonial discourse produces a slippage, a textual surplus between the demand of colonialism for reformed subjects and what it desires in return: a reform only up to a certain threshold that if colonial subjects were to pass through, there would then be no way of distinguishing between the identities of, for example, English and Indian or friend and enemy. This minimal gap between the demand and desire that constitutes the colonial subject, then, is the very moment of rhetorical invention that constitutes Englishness in the first place. I read this trace of surplus textuality as disinvention and suggest that the grounds of politics can read otherwise from this surplus.

Pérez understands the interstice of history as an ontological gap that can be remedied by unmasking discourse to reveal a truth. The concept of the decolonial imaginary, then, serves as the method for the critical practice of restitution and, further, for deconstructing the "European and Euroamerican historical method" and for "going outside [this method] in order to come back with different kinds of inquires."[5] "Traditional historiographical categories," Pérez argues, "questioned only from within for revision, have been built upon that which came before, and therefore have contributed to the colonial. The categories themselves are exclusive, in that they already deny and negate the voice of the other." On the other hand, Pérez contends that the decolonial imaginary arises in the "interstitial gaps [that] interrupt the linear model of time, and it is in such locations that oppositional, subaltern histories can be found": "Foucault's redefinition of archaeology, understood as a method, disrupts linear continuity to locate silences within the interstices. . . . I argue that these silences, when heard, become the negotiating spaces for the decolonizing subject. It is in a sense where third space agency is articulated. . . . This new category, the decolonial imaginary, can help us to rethink history in a way that makes Chicana/o agency transformative."[6]

The Decolonial Imaginary hinges on a conceptualization of alterity as a supplement to the category of history: both a negative part that was added to make history complete (the interstice *is* the antithesis that is the very condition of possibility for hegemonic synthesis) *and* the part added to replace history that was assumed to be already complete (that is, the interstice is assumed to be self-evident and, therefore, a positive element of history). The category of the decolonial imaginary is therefore marked by the absence that supplements. Nevertheless, just like Western history, the decolonial imaginary is always inhabited by a certain exorbitance that must produce alterity as a supplement.

The Rhetorical Imaginary

I'd like to read *The Decolonial Imaginary* with Krista Ratcliffe's widely cited *Rhetorical Listening: Identification, Gender, Whiteness* to engage in a bit of "disciplinary exposure," as I mentioned in the introduction. In addition to providing an outstanding complication of the trope of race in U.S.-American discourse and the ways in which to think about "troubled [racial and gendered] identifications," Rattcliffe frames racial and gendered difference as descriptive categories that are not representational.[7] In seeking out a new way of thinking about cross-cultural communication, Ratcliffe proposes a strategy of rhetorical listening, which she defines as "a trope for interpretive invention, that is, [a] stance of openness that a person may choose to assume in relation to any person, text, or culture; its purpose is to cultivate conscious identifications in ways that promote productive communication, especially but not solely cross-culturally."[8] Listening, Ratcliffe argues, is a means for rendering alterity intelligible so that one can negotiate (invent responses to) the logocentrism constituting antagonistic cross-cultural encounters.

Anticipating the critiques of her framework, Ratcliffe, positions listening against poststructuralism:

> Although poststructuralist theory calls such differences into question, it has inadvertently served as a third disciplinary bias in our field's neglect of listening. Jacques Derrida's project to deconstruct Western metaphysics reverses Plato's celebration of speaking and suspicion of writing. Consequently, deconstruction champions writing as a trope that more accurately describes textuality, or how we use language and how language uses us. Moreover, it collapses reading into this equation by arguing that writing is reading is writing. But because it designates speaking as the trope that fosters a metaphysics of presence, poststructuralist theory in the wake of Derrida finds itself suspicious of speaking and, by association, of listening, even though Derrida pays tribute to listening as a means of substituting the ethical for the ideal in his essay about Emmanuel Levinas. But even as Derrida flirts with listening, his focus is on reading: As Christie McDonald claims in her preface to Derrida's *Ear of the Other*, "what is at stake in [his] vast program is contemporary *reading* and how it becomes possible to assume political positions."[9]

What seems to be at issue here is not simply reading's incommensurability with listening but listening's incommensurability with writing. Still, both speech and writing are called into question by Derrida, and metaphysical concepts cannot be solved through an appeal to unity—which is the goal of rhetorical listening. For Ratcliffe, rhetorical listening amounts to a trope of cross-cultural communication, different from the act of reading. Still, it is this subject identity/difference binary that provides the grounds for Western metaphysics and logocentrism. This same nonrepresentational identity/difference problematic emerges when Ratcliffe outlines the necessary conditions for an ethics of rhetorical listening: "First a listener must be imagined with an agency that enables him or her to choose to act ethically, either by listening and/or by acting upon that listening.... Second, given this agency, listeners must be provided with a lexicon and tactics for listening and for acting upon their listening."[10] At issue here is Ratcliffe's separation of reading from textuality (writing) on the grounds that one signifies reception and the other production. It is unclear how one is to determine the difference between reading and listening. Furthermore, how is reading *not* textuality?

Ratcliffe proposes a model for conceptualizing the Other without recourse to ontology and states the telos of rhetorical listening as follows:

> By posing understanding [of self and other] as an end of rhetorical listening, I am not proposing that we idealize understanding or authorial intent: My purpose is neither to promote a "textual realism" wherein a text is perceived as a repository of *the* truth nor to celebrate a naïve "readerly idealism" wherein the contexts of speakers/writers are simplified and the contexts of reader/listeners erased. Rather, my purpose is . . . to collapse the real/ideal dichotomy into a strategic third ground where rhetorical negotiation is exposed as always already existing and where rhetorical listening is posited as one means of that negotiation.
>
> Granted, such a purpose resonates with remnants of idealism. But, as mentioned earlier, I like to consider these remnants strategic. Just as Gayatri Spivak justifies subalterns' employing a "*strategic* essentialism" in their critique of postcolonial oppression . . . I am advocating a strategic idealism when listening with the intent to understand.[11]

Ultimately, rhetorical listening is predicated on generating understanding by bypassing representation in the process of communication. For this to happen, the other has to become an exteriority by which an intellectual practices self-reflexive critique. The other, therefore, reflects back to the intellectual the positive qualities lacking in the intellectual, thus becoming a constitutive element in an economy of reading in which the other marks the limit of institutional (interior) reason. This constitutive exteriority—meaning, beyond the limits of hegemonic reason—is then *understood* as the speech of an other. This appears in Ratcliffe's invocation of *nepantla* as a grounding for rhetorical invention, which she cites to argue that listening is not the opposite of silence but the act of invention for imagining spaces in between hegemonic binaries.

Furthermore, rhetorical listening hinges on the opposition of a good writing versus bad writing, represented by writing qua listening (good) and writing qua writing (bad). If, as Ratcliffe claims, listening transmutates hearing into invention, reception into production, it will not have been because "rhetorical listening turns *intent* back on the listener, focusing on listening with intent to hear troubled identifications"; rather, it will be simply because listening means reading (writing) produces meaning (writing). Nothing about this is nonrepresentational.[12] The appeal to exteriority as the evidence and confirmation of difference constitutes a movement of the sign in writing and not in subjects themselves. While her definition emphasizes the role of the audience in developing meaning with the speaker and while nonetheless framing meaning and identity as socially situated, it is the location of difference in rhetorical listening that still comes from *across* an internally constituted exteriority. There is no room for difference to emerge from *within* a sign system or "cultural logic" itself since "[as] a trope for interpretive invention, rhetorical listening differs from reading in that it proceeds via different body organs, different disciplinary and cultural assumptions, different figures of speech, and most importantly different stances."[13] Despite this, however, in rhetorical listening, there is a most interesting epistemic ambivalence when we hear that invention has two meanings—(1) invention (reading, listening) in the sense of hermeneutical meaning-making as re-presenting and (2) invention in the sense of representations of the other conjured for the hermeneutic process—in the latter of which there is a mark left by an exorbitant rhetoricity.

I am arguing here that both the decolonial imaginary and rhetorical listening are framed as interpretive acts that eschew ideological and representative processes by appealing to topoi of exteriority to Western power/knowledge. My goal in reading these frames together is not to post them as examples of a critical deficiency, nor is it to supplant these frames with my own as superior.

Instead, and following Graff Zivin, my goal is to build an indisciplined conversation "in which we would begin to think new concepts—weak, erroneous concepts—of ethics and politics, in which we privilege thought, thinking over university knowledge."[14] The decolonial imaginary and rhetorical listening are critical frames that are produced by and against Western modernity—and by and against university knowledge. In the exposure of these frames to each other, appeals to topoi of exteriority resemble what Derrida describes "as the first exteriority in general, the enigmatic relationship of the living to its other and of an inside to an outside: spacing." A spatial exterior, Derrida writes, "would not appear without the grammé, without difference as temporalization, without the nonpresence of the other inscribed within the sense of the present, without the relationship with death as the concrete structure of the living present."[15] A non-Western exteriority bears positive meaning only as a negative quality of what it is not.

Posthegemonic Rupture

I turn now to read a historiography of critical thought that reworks this spatial ambivalence as a critical resource. Alberto Moreiras describes two registers of Latinamericanist thought. First-order Latinamericanism is "an epistemic machine in charge of representing the Latin American difference" and "aspires to a particular form of disciplinary power that it inherits from the imperialist state apparatus."[16] Pérez, for example, suggests that the topos of the historical interstice inaugurates an entirely new consciousness altogether, "issuing a 'new' postnationalist project in which *la nueva mestiza*, the mixed-race woman, is the privileged subject of an interstitial space that was formerly a nation, and is now without borders, without boundaries."[17] Mestizaje is proposed as the essence of bordered space, as the result of mixture, and as the very ontological process by which the category of politics emerges. The interstice, the border itself, is a political gap in addition to its role as the historical gap. Pérez grounds the border in the discourse of mestizaje, given that Pérez reads the category of new mestiza consciousness as the interstitial or borderlands consciousness from which to "write the 'other' without making the 'other' the same or placing the 'other' within the same."[18] Pérez wagers that the space of borderlands—or, rather, the consequences of mixture (supposedly the creation of smooth space) that borderlands exemplifies—"[introduces] the possibility of a postcolonial, postnational consciousness."[19] Now, the interstice becomes the site of the political—the site of hegemonic incompletion, which in her terms signifies a deterritorialization brought about by mestizaje in postnational times.

Mestizo cultural identity has come to be thought of as the basis of freedom (from colonization, from nation-state hegemony) because it is assumed to be an impure, heterogeneous identity that impurifies any grounding of politics in racial purity. But this form of thought is itself a new form of purity. It has one of its paradigmatic roots in Gloria Anzaldúa's *Borderlands/La Frontera*, a massively important text that figures border space (borderlands) as the site of mixture where a new mestiza consciousness is produced. Anzaldúa writes, "At the confluence of two or more genetic streams, . . . this mixture of races, rather than resulting in an inferior being, provides hybrid progeny, a mutable, more malleable species with a rich gene pool."[20] For Anzaldúa, borderlands are a site of rhetorical invention for determining who belongs and who does not. Indeed, over the past twenty-five years, critics have enlisted enunciations from the locus of borderlands to fashion political critique from a new mestiza consciousness as a form of critique that avoids the traps of Western essentialism and universalism.

There is a kind of slippage in one necessary and axiological part of *Borderlands'* articulation. At the core of its edifice is an oppositional structure that proposes to produces a de-essentializing or nonessential subject position from which to critique essentializing and universalizing discourses. However, in both formal and political terms, its counterhegemonic, rhetorical force is grounded by an assumption of an essence that it cannot get rid of. *Borderlands*, in other words, is just as invested in a certain kind of purity as it is in resisting other kinds. There is a triple mark at the intersection of politics and identity in *Borderlands/La Frontera*: (1) a petition for intelligibility, which (2) requires unintelligibility of someone else, which therefore articulates (3) a modified sovereign exception, which produces a thinking of politics as the administration of community on the Schmittian basis of friend/enemy *and yet* mandates the restitution of the excluded. Let me read Anzaldúa's explanation of how an identity of mixture forms the ground of a consciousness at the end of history itself:

> The new *mestiza* copes by developing a tolerance for contradictions, a tolerance for ambiguity. She learns to be an Indian in Mexican culture, to be Mexican from an Anglo point of view. . . . Not only does she sustain contradictions, she turns the ambivalence into something else. She can be

jarred out of ambivalence by an intense, and often painful, emotional event which inverts or resolves the ambivalence. I'm not sure exactly how. The work takes place underground—subconsciously. It is the work that the soul performs. The focal point or fulcrum, that juncture where the *mestiza* stands, is where phenomena tend to collide. It is where the possibility of uniting all that is separate occurs. This assembly is not one where severed pieces merely come together. Nor is it a balancing of opposing powers. In attempting to work out a synthesis, the self has added a third element which is greater than the sum of its severed parts. The third element is a new consciousness—a *mestiza* consciousness—and though it is a source of intense pain, its energy comes from continual creative motion that keeps breaking down the unitary aspect of each new paradigm. *En unas pocas centurias* the future will belong to the mestiza because the future depends on the breaking down of paradigms, it depends on the straddling of two or more cultures. By creating a new mythos—that is a change in the way we perceive reality, the way we see ourselves, and the way we behave—*la mestiza* creates a new consciousness.[21]

In formal terms, Anzaldúa negates a number of hierarchies by questioning and rejecting the idea of essence as grounds for authority by appealing to a de-essentializing mixture. Anzaldúa's theory of mestiza consciousness is robust and has generated useful frameworks for the study of rhetorical invention. Still, if mestizaje bears the mark of a certain collision, even beyond a mere unification of severed pieces, it still nevertheless bears the mark of a preexisting set. And, in formal terms, even if mestizaje describes an assemblage as opposed to a mere collection such that a new consciousness *emerges* as the result of continual interaction between component parts, the structural operation of mixture itself, which is always antecedent, its set of component parts must remain unquestioned for hybridization to take place. One could re-mark the passage "the future will belong to the mestiza because the future depends on the breaking down of paradigms" to inscribe its tautology: "the future will belong to the mestiza because [the future is hybrid]."

This appeal to futurity brings us to an uncomfortable claim to origin. Anzaldúa outlines the hegemony of the mestiza with three main moves: the argument that the authentic mestizo has legitimate claim to the U.S. Southwest geopolitic; the conflation of the mestiza with Indigeneity writ large; and the claim that the mestiza has an essential condition of resistance to colonial power.

In other words, throughout the text, Anzaldúa argues that the mestiza has claim to the U.S. Southwest, is mestiza (read: of Mexican ancestry), and is always subhegemonic. No other subject can fit this mold.

As Acosta points out, for Anzaldúa, the figure of *los recién llegados*, migrants who have successfully crossed the border from northern Mexico and brought with them a northern Mexican dialect, serve as the figure of a heterogeneous or nonessentialist discourse from which she postulates a negation of the existing hegemonic order. *Los recién llegados*, in other words, are cited as evidence of the essential quality of the Borderlands: the mixture between *los recién llegados* (outsiders) and U.S.-Americans and Mexican Americans (insiders) that produces heterogeneous forms of subjectivity and signification and that demonstrates the impropriety of cultural and linguistic purity. Anzaldúa makes this idea clear in the following passage:

> *Nosotros los* Chicanos straddle the borderlands. On one side, of us, we are constantly exposed to the Spanish of the Mexicans, on the other side we hear the Anglos' incessant clamoring so that we forget our language. Among ourselves we don't say *nosotros los americanos, o nosotros los españoles, o nosotros los hispanos*. We say *nosotros los mexicanos* (by *mexicanos* we do not mean citizens of Mexico; we do not mean a national identity, but a racial one). . . . Deep in our hearts we believe that being Mexican has nothing to do with which country one lives in. Being Mexican is a state of soul—not one of mind, not one of citizenship. Neither eagle nor serpent, but both. And like the ocean, neither animal respects borders.[22]

Anzaldúa argues that the mestiza subject holds a geopolitical claim to the U.S. Southwest and that this legitimacy grants the mestiza subject an exceptional position with which to counter Western colonization. In the chapter titled "The Homeland, Aztlán/El Otro Mexico," Anzaldúa describes the migration of mestizas from south to north, back to the homeland they had left behind centuries ago. She writes, "Today we are witnessing la migracion de los pueblos Mexicanos, the return odyssey to the historical/mythological Aztlán. This time, the traffic is from south to north" and "This land was Mexican once/was indian always/and is/And will be again."[23] Thus, Anzaldúa bases her argument for the rights and recognition of mestizas on an ontology of place. Although the topos of origin of *El Plan Espiritual de Aztlán*, for example, and *Borderlands/La Frontera* has helped inspire and organize political consciousness, Anzaldúa's ancestral claim to Aztlán implies the entitlement of mestizas to land that has been already become occupied. Furthermore, ascribing the U.S. Southwest only to mestizas and focusing solely on their historical claim obscures the heterogeneous effects of a multifaceted European colonization that produced arrays of subalternity for Native peoples.

Gareth Williams demonstrates how this mode of thinking constituted the basis of nation-state hegemony, as it constituted the very category of the people *itself* as a heterogeneous mixture around which to construct identities of resistance to the West and the North. In his reading of transculturation during the national-popular epoch in Latin America, Williams reads transculturation in two distinct but related registers: transculturation as the material condition of exchange obtaining within postcolonial conditions, and transculturation as a rhetoric of politics: "if we distinguish between transculturation as a heterogeneous cultural ensemble and transculturation as a desire and an intellectual discourse; and if we do this as a means of viewing the thought of transculturation in relation to the formation of institutional structures, political identities, state apparatuses, and intellectual interventions into the public sphere . . . , then in transculturation we encounter not only the popular forms of self-expression and differential modes of collective self-definition but also an immensely powerful ideological machinery of which popular expressions of difference are often merely little more than an effect."[24] The threshold between these domains of transculturation not only corresponds to the antagonism that hegemony theory is supposed to describe (the formation of subjects from above [state] or change from below [people]), but more important, it renders clear the problem inhabiting the core of intellectual desire—its indistinction from capitalist modernization in the region. If the category of the popular emerges as a material condition *and* an idea during a period in Latin America in which cultural elites were thinking about politics as a process of change from below (and as a means of integrating peasant classes into a national public sphere), then it's hard to imagine how the intellectual desire for popular incorporation from below can be said to operate beyond the state's calculation and mobilization of the people as the grounds of its own legitimacy. Or in Williams's words, by reflecting on transculturation in both registers, "we can approach transculturation not merely as a positive culturalism but, more problematically, as a privileged discourse in the consolidation and often violent expansion of the Creole state's hegemony over national territories, populations, and classes."[25]

What is at stake with first-order Latinamericanism, in the appeal to an exteriority that would serve as the location of the limit of Western thinking and the inauguration of a new subject of difference that is nevertheless intelligible to university thought, is an ontological figuration of difference as A ≠ B. What is at stake in this maintenance of difference? What would happen, in other words, if A = B?

Furthermore, in this ontology of difference, there is an exorbitance, marked by an injunction both to draw the limit of the West on the basis of difference and, at the same time, to constitute a new community on the basis of this difference. Is this not the very move that *The Decolonial Imaginary* disavows with the declaration of a postnational condition as the end of Western thought? Can identity function as the grounds of both legitimacy and illegitimacy? *The Decolonial Imaginary* is, of course, not the first to suggest, from the topos of border, that nation-state hegemony is experiencing a fundamental restructuring in the wake of globalization, which, in turn, prompts more questions about the possibility of reading culture in a historical moment defined by a crisis in nation-state hegemony.[26] And, while critics agree that nation-state hegemony in the region has experienced a fundamental shift in relation to globalization, they disagree on the effects such a shift has on politics and possibilities for critical reflection in postnational times.

In response, Moreiras wonders, "What is then the type of historical imagination that could warrant a reformulation of the project of critical reason as a properly politico-epistemological project? In other words, where can we find a force for intrasystemic irruption if the system has expanded in such a way that no productive notion of an outside is permitted?"[27] To answer this question is to reflect first on the will to know in a context where "no productive notion of an outside is permitted." It requires a meditation on politics from a surplus of the social text that cannot be recovered to produce more governmentality. This "impossibility" to establish a plat from the perspective of subalternity is infrastructural, for subalternity is merely the subject effect of the differential movement conditioned by any rhetorical choice. Recall the ambivalence that *The Decolonial Imaginary* exhibited toward the interstice: the interstice became the name for the absence of historical substance, of which *la nueva mestiza* serves as supplement. If Latinamericanism in its first order relied on the conceptualization of the interstice in terms of its spatial restitution, second-order Latinamericanism promotes the role of excess to the condition of possibility for thinking the infrastructural transformation of hegemonic interpellation altogether: "That is, no longer as the possibility of turning a dominated ideology into the domi-nant but rather as the possibility of thinking the outside of hegemony: posthe-gemonic thinking."[28]

Posthegemony is an attempt to think publicity, public space itself, at the absolute limit of hegemonic interpellation, for what comes after the democratic rupture remains yet to arrive. Posthegemony is a rhetorical project that remains productive only as a permanent, affirmative critique of the negative. The differ-ence between first-order Latinamericanism's *outside* and the second order's *beyond* is subtle, but the latter points to an incongruence between the institu-tionalization of cultural politics and an always deferred site of subaltern excess: a given formation of sheer unreadability in a text that points to the incomple-tion of any form of intellectual practice and, therefore, the possibility of rethink-ing the relation of intellectual practice itself to the political. This formation structural incompletion is not an identity or consciousness but the residue of signification that interpellation will always fail to capture. By definition, hege-mony not only is incomplete but presupposes the lack of its own grounding, which is why signification and interpellation are phenomena in the first place.[29] Latinamericanism in its second order is an approach to the thinking of politics from the inevitable structural excess of the hegemony-subalternity relation itself. Posthegemony is a practice of asserting that politics can be thought beyond the incessant reduction of politics to a choice between Eurocentrism and mestizaje. A response to Moreiras's question lies in determining the role of critical thought in a historical moment in which the university as a civic institu-tion can no longer be said to operate outside market enforcement, which, as critics have noted, might have always been the telos of the nation-state.

Williams foregrounds the wane of the national-popular (national-revolutionary) after Latin America's insertion into globalized capital. Analyzing "the even, incomplete, and ongoing passage from national to postnational cultural and political paradigms in Latin America," Williams argues that "transnationaliza-tion and the insertion of Latin American nations into global networks has ungrounded the nation-state and, alongside it, the transformational potential of the national-popular. It has brought the nation-state and the national-popular (Gramsci's 'nation-people') to their economic, institutional, and conceptual knees. Therefore, through increasing transnationalization, we are living the historical 'other side' of the national-popular; the (collapsed/collapsing) side of the people; the national-popular in its state of exhaustion and redistribution across regional and national frontiers."[30] For Williams, the postnational does not signify the end of the nation-state form but its recombination in the wake of neoliberal development, which rendered a shift in hegemonic models in the region. Latin America's insertion into global circulation undermined the grounding and constitutive element of cultural and social hegemonies in discretely bordered Latin American nations: the national/popular antagonism. Whereas hegemony, in the national/popular antagonism, functioned to enable the articulation of a universalizing national project through the constitution of distinct spatial exteriorities (with, for example, national frontiers), globalization set in motion a generalized spatial crisis—a generalized condition of the wane of previously functional topoi for emancipatory politics such as "the people."

Williams is not the first to give the name "posthegemony" to the wane of the national/popular period in Latin America. In "Civil Society, Consumption, and Governmentality in an Age of Global Restructuring," George Yúdice contends that the emergence of globalization corresponds with an erosion of the dialectical mediation of state and civil domains, which, he suggests, demonstrates a condition of new forms of hegemonic mediation and capital accumulation. Yúdice conceives of this in the following terms: "Flexible accumulation, consumer culture, and the 'new world information order' are produced or distributed (made to flow) globally, to occupy the space of the nation, but are no longer 'motivated' by any essential connection to a state, as embodied, for example, in a 'national-popular' formation. Their motivations are both infra- and supranational. We might say that, from the purview of the national proscenium, a posthegemonic situation holds. That is, the 'compromise solution' that culture provided for Gramsci is not now one that pertains to the national level but to the local and transnational."[31] In opposition to Michael Hardt's conclusion that "not the State, but civil society has withered away!" Yúdice links the state/civil antagonism *together* as a hegemonic form augmented by flexible accumulation.[32] Yúdice suggests that flexible accumulation incites a shift in the relation of state sovereignty to global capital, a claim that reworks Antonio Gramsci's assumption that when the state is finally unseated or "reabsorbed" by the counterhegemonic force of civil society, "a sturdy structure of civil society [will be] at once revealed."[33] For Yúdice, then, posthegemony is the name for the condition in which flexible accumulation has taken its seat as *the* structure of civil society, a condition in which global capital, not the nation-state, saturates the field of social relations. The key phrase here—*flexible accumulation is made to flow*—signals a change in the nation-state's form. It is not that the international border, for example, has been razed but that the function of the border changes. If the

concept of the border was once a form of segmentation and restriction in disciplinary society, then perhaps the border serves as a threshold in which flexible
accumulation is now *made* (forced) to flow.[34] If this is the case, and the nature of
the border has shifted in response to the restructuring of the nation-state, how
is it possible that the interstitial border can serve as the site of any political
resistance to global capital?

What is at stake in the question of posthegemony is an "opening up of the
political field to a certain form of unintelligibility," an alterity whose negativity
marks not only the incompletion of global capital but also an opening to a
rhetoricity that will have never been overdetermined by university thought—
to a locus of rhetorical invention still yet to arrive.[35] To return to Moreiras's
question, then, Is it possible to engage a thought of politics in such a way that
no productive notion of an outside is permitted? I answer this question by
"regarding," in Michelle Ballif's words, or "guarding," in Graff Zivin's, a disinvention immanent to Latinamericanism as a weak force that cannot apprehend
and provides a means to trace democracy on that part that is always deferred
and therefore impossible to incorporate.[36] In a formal sense, insofar as the sign
"Latin America" designates a supplement to Europe, Latinamericanism
becomes a reflection on the problem of the proper account itself and therefore
undermines the logic of the false choice of Eurocentrism/mestizaje from which
it withdraws.

Undocumenting

I observe such a political opening in Guillermo Gómez-Peña's performance art.
Originally published in 1998 as a performance text and later, in 2000, as a trade
book, *Codex Espangliensis: From Columbus to Border Patrol* narrates the conquest of the Americas in reverse, recounting violent events from the constitutive
encounter between European and Amerindian groups to the institutionaliza-
tion of global capital in the North American Free Trade Agreement. *Codex*
appears decisive in its narration of encounters at different borders, given that
blood runs through nearly every page as a visual trope, and it appears that
despite the direction in which one reads this historical fact—whether forward
or reverse, Europe to Latin America or Latin America to Europe, hegemonic or
counterhegemonic—one cannot escape the violence that mediates cultural
exchange. And, while the bulk of the text is focused on the reimagination of a

cartography of domination in counterhegemonic fashion, it is the event of the encounter on which a disinvention is at work.

Critics read *Codex* as a formalization of a new hybrid, mestizo cultural identity from which to formalize a counterhegemonic thought and imagine new modes of political community. *Codex* could be read, as Damián Baca contends, as the hybrid result of the mixture of two previously existing forms of cultural production: "By fusing and embellishing Mesoamerican pictography into European inscription practices, Mestiz@ codex rhetorics promote a new dialectic, a new strategy of inventing and writing between worlds."[37] Additionally, Lisa Wolford describes Gómez-Peña's art as the production of "the Fourth World": "it is a space that privileges hybridity and calls into question ascribed boundaries of identity and community, a realm in which binaristic conceptions of self and other collapse and implode."[38] It is perhaps valid to read *Codex* as Gómez-Peña articulating a hybrid identity and the hybrid group identities of which he is a part to finally produce a level of intelligibility that would qualify them for inclusion into the categories of history, citizenship, and so on. Additionally, for Franny Howes, "*Codex Espangliensis* is a massive act of memory, reaching into both American popular cultural imagery and indigenous imagery to invent a way to represent the ongoing struggles of colonialism in a way that is both new and old."[39] Kat Austin and Carlos-Urani Montiel read *Codex Espangliensis* as the product of hybridity—as evidence of the "Chicana/o mind" and the political space of the U.S.-Mexico border, arguing that the "cultural negotiations and the distinct consciousness that emerges in their wake constitute the crucial components of a border identity that may provide the necessary threads for uniting a diverse community for the purpose of resistance."[40] In similar fashion, Cruz Medina reads the codex as a production of "the cultural mestizaje of border art and rhetoric."[41]

These readings take the event of encounter as the constitutive moment of mixture—as the production of a new form of subject and, in turn, the production of a new form of politics. The event is the encounter between incommensurate groups, violent conquest. The mestizo subject, in its first order, is a hybrid subject, the result of mixture. And yet what is exceptional about this subject is that which is *beyond* it—the exceptional quality is not necessarily *of* the subject but something that arrives and forcefully constitutes it. It inherits a force of violence. The politics of mestizaje is grounded in a violence that it must reproduce as its condition of possibility.

Whether this event occurs in forward or reverse, what is important here is the hybrid condition proceeding from the force of violence. The first axiom of mestizo identification is that the mestizo subject is constituted in an act of mixture grounded in the condition of violence. The second axiom of mestizo identity is, "I mix; therefore, I am" (the force of the reason of the strongest). Gómez-Peña's denarrativizes the event in reverse:

> in 1492, an
> AZTEC SAILOR
> NAMED NOCTLI
> EUROPZIN TEZPOCA
> DEPARTED FROM THE
> PORT OF MINATITLAN
> with a small flotilla of
> wooden rafts. 3 months later
> HE DISCOVERED A NEW
> CONTINENT AND NAMED IT
> EUROPZIN AFTER HIMSELF.
> In November 1512, the
> OMNI-POTENT AZTECS BEGAN
> THE CONQUEST OF *EUROPZIN*
> IN THE NAME OF THY FATHER
> TEZCATLIPOCA, LORD OF CROSS-
> CULTURAL MISUNDERSTANDINGS
> y entonces el desmadre se comenzo a multiplicar
> logo-rhythmically and logo- aritmicamente[42]

Here, I cite the performance poem "Califas," from which an excerpt appears in and lends narrative to *Codex Espangliensis*. "Califas" is reproduced nearly verbatim in *Codex Espangliensis*, except for sentence casing, spacing, and the replacement of "misconceptions" with "misunderstandings." I do this for the sake of accuracy or perhaps to reflect on accuracy as motif of *Codex Espangliensis*. The text is replete with cross-cultural misunderstandings. The process of mixture never produces accurate understandings of subjectivity in pre-Columbian or post-Columbian times.

From *Codex Espangliensis*, however, it's possible to misunderstand the law of mestizaje by way of reading a disinvention between location and name. Conquest is the event that sets hybridity in motion. It's a violent force constituting mestizo subjectivity. If this constitutive force can be narrated in reverse—that is, applied to the other—then one can reason that mestizaje can be dissociated from location. Perhaps it would be possible, then, to mark mestizo subjectivity in a generic sense, as differential, given that what constitutes mestizo subjectivity is an event that arrives and inaugurates a value of difference-from-(insert proper name here). In other words, *Codex Espangliensis* narrates the formation of mestizo subjectivity in Europe, where Europeans, too, can be marked under the heading of mestizaje. Remember, the law of mestizaje states only the axiomatic mixture between European/Amerindian. Nowhere does it specify a location clause— that it can only occur in the landmass named Latin America. As such, I observe a Latinamericanism without Latin America, a Latinamericanism in the most generic sense—a Latinamericanism at the place where the metaphysics of the subject breaks down.

I read in *Codex Espangliensis* a momentary loss of commonplace, a disinvention between location and name where the sign "Latin America" shorts out. And, even if coloniality did not happen in reverse and even if its reversal would be impossible, *Codex Espangliensis* nevertheless produces an exorbitant ambivalence of the sign "Latin America," which has always circulated value beyond the landmass that the sign itself signifies. "Latin America" has always been marked as a constitutive exteriority, and as such, it is redundant to ground resistance to the West in the metaphysics of a mestizo subject, for the mestizo subject was always already Western.

Codex Espangliensis provides an opportunity to reflect on what political activity means, at least in the definition posed by Rancière: as "whatever shifts a body from the place assigned to it or changes a place's destination." For Rancière, politics is not the name for a mode of governmentality but, rather, the name for the rupture of governmentality that might pass itself off as democracy. Rancière contends, "Any subjectification is a disidentification, removal from the naturalness of a place, the opening up of a subject space where anyone can be counted."[43] Mestizaje, in its generic, second-order sense, becomes political when anyone at all can participate as a mestizo subject. In an interview with Gómez-Peña, Eduardo Mendieta asked him about stakes of this generic opening:

> **Mendieta:** Are you suggesting that the discourses of difference have been already co-opted and have therefore become passé—even de rigueur and establishment—and thus perhaps suspect?

Gómez-Peña: The subjects of identity politics are passé. We are already installed in a postracist/postsexist society. They want sexy images of race and hybridity, but without the text. Unlike their multicultural or post-colonial predecessors, the new impresarios and self-proclaimed experts of Otherness are no longer interested in the tensions and clashes of cultures. They no longer wish to discuss issues of power and privilege. They know better. They don't want their neocolonial positionality questioned by angry primitives and strident women. They suffer from the Vietnam syndrome of the cultural wars. Besides, what they really want is to market Otherness, not to understand it. What the impresarios of globalization want is mild salsa and tofu tamales. They want Zapatista supermodels, not "real" Zapatistas. They want Salma Hayek to play Frida Kahlo. They want "Livin' la Vida Loca" sung by Ricky Martin, not enacted by gang members. . . . In this respect, the pertinent question for performance artists is, How do we continue raising crucial issues without scaring our audiences or without facing deportation back to the margins? My answer, for the moment, is that we must mimic mainstream culture, and when the mirror is standing between them and us, reflecting their fantasies and desires, we break it in the audience's face. If parts of the mirror get in their eyes, that's their problem.[44]

What does it mean to have race and hybridity without the text? Perhaps that to which Žižek refers as the total rearticulation of politics without politics: "On today's market, we find a whole series of products deprived of their malignant property: coffee without caffeine, cream without fat, beer without alcohol."[45] Are the market and the university not indistinct in offering a generalized form of flexible accumulation, which is to say, the consumption of identity without its malignancies (a Zapatista without the peasant, on the one hand, and a [hybrid] identity without difference, on the other)? What we have here is two sides of a double injunction: if first-order university thought is constituted by the injunction to both reduce and preserve alterity, with global capital we get the injunction to reduce and preserve the national frontiers that produce a forced migration of cultural forms. If globalized capital and university thought obtain as a false choice, should one not, instead, locate the moment that smashes the mirror and sends a shard into the eye?

If Latinamericanism conceives of itself as a form of antiglobal intellectual practice through claims of an irreducible geographical and critical distance from the global, and if the subjects and objects of study that it holds within its conceptual domain no longer reside on the other side of a set of neatly articulated national, cultural, and political borders—subjects and objects that were held to represent and demonstrate not only difference itself but the possibility for a locus of antiglobalist thought—in *Codex* one is confronted to think through the movement of this difference back into the Iberian metropole. In other words, if these subjects and objects were understood to represent difference because they were located beyond the reaches of the metropole, are we now to understand that they are no longer different and therefore no longer representative of antiglobalist thought? No. On the contrary, in *Codex* one is confronted with an imagination of subjects as that which "denarrativize" the structural connection of history to logic (and of place to name) on disinvention.[46] The disinvention in *Codex* is the moment when mestizaje can be read democratically—that is, as undocumented, removed from its placement as natural in Latin America.

As the moment of hegemonic failure in *Codex*, the disinvention of the encounter event is a speech issued from without place—a place not yet named or yet to arrive in intelligibility—whose translation into the conventional account of knowledge would be impossible. It is in this disinvention that a rupture happens. Žižek refers to this rupture as a preeminent democratic act: the eruption of a new mode of thought from which a previous regime was constituted. One might now be able to read the encounter event against itself—that is, against its first-order Latinamericanist conscription into service as the ground of politics—as a moment in *Codex* in which one witnesses "the struggle about the field of struggle itself," where the assertion that the encounter is always a miscount becomes an assertion that, as of yet, there exists no topos through which to mediate a new community based on subject position.[47]

Another example from Gómez-Peña's performance art is *Documentado/ Undocumented Ars Shamánica Performática* (2017), a collaborative multimedia, performance text framed as a portable altar in the spirit of Marcel Duchamp's *Boîte-en-Valise* (1948). The text includes a conversation between Gómez-Peña and a "radical nativist" in which they discuss the issue of "illegal" immigration in the United States. Gómez-Peña argues that immigration is an ethical issue rather than a legal issue. His use of Spanglish generates ambivalence and a disinvention in the certainty of both English and Spanish as markers of identity or difference that, similar to *Codex Espangliensis*, forms a politics unmoored from geopolitical origin.

In a section of the codex titled "we are here because you were there," Gómez-Peña describes a conversation with a "radical nativist" who engages him on the topic of "illegal" immigration in the United States, which I quote at length:

> During a recent debate I had with a radical nativist, he asked me to provide him with a strong reason why the US should not entirely close its borders with Mexico.
>
> My answer was as follows:
>
> "To me, the 'problem' is not immigration . . . it's immigration hysteria.
>
> Immigration is a byproduct of globalization and as such, it is irreversible. One-third of mankind now lives outside our homeland and away from our original culture and language." His face was blank. (*I pass my hand over my face*)
>
> "The existing nation/states are dysfunctional & outdated. And the legal structures that contain them do not respond to the new complexities of the times."
>
> His response to my answer was: "I don't understand a word of what you are saying. The fact is that the aliens are here illegally."
>
> Hmm . . . I held my tongue and continued in the same Chicano-cool-mono-tone I use when I'm getting pissed:
>
> "Illegally? . . . To me immigration is not a legal issue but a humanistic & ethical one. No human being is 'illegal,' period. All human beings, with or without documents, belong to humankind, our kind, and if they require our help, we are obliged to provide it. It's called being human—a concept you may find quite 'alien' & 'foreign' in itself. In this context, nationality becomes secondary. Their pain is ours, and so is their fate."
>
> "What do you mean by that?" he asked contentiously.
>
> "Just as I became an immigrant one day, you yourself might become one in the future. We are all potential immigrants, carnal."
>
> He looked at me with disgust and after a long pause, he said, "Don't give me this 'carnal' shit. You people are determined to destroy our democracy, just because we give you the freedom to do it. What have WE done to YOU?"
>
> At that point I realized that there was not much space for intellectual negotiation with him. His arguments were strictly emotional. He was fighting for his life, his inner country, and his sense of belonging to an imaginary world, a pre-contact White America that never was. He was

the real alien, lost in a multiracial & multicultural foreign planet where border culture and hybridity are the norm, and Spanglish is the lingua franca.

I felt compassion for him. I tried once more to engage him in a serious dialogue:

"You know, ese . . ."

"Don't talk to me in Spanish!"

"You know, sir, in response to your question of what have we done to you: immigration to the US is the direct result of the economic & political behavior of the US toward other countries. We are here precisely because you were there. Most immigrants, including myself, are unconsciously searching for the source of our despair. And I think I found it just now, located in your historical amnesia. It's a pleasure to meet you."[48]

At first glance, it would appear that Gómez-Peña's claim of Spanglish as lingua franca displaces the radical nativist's romanticization of a monolingual nation-state.[49] This would make sense, given that such a claim would appear to disrupt an ideological formation that Nelson Flores and Jonathan Rosa identify as a perpetual inappropriateness of Spanish, which reflects the "raciolinguistic" exceptionalism of a standardized English in the United States.[50] However, this claim might also be read as a disinvention that traces these oppositions (English/Spanish) to a point of indistinction, where such perceived differences are merely the effect of exchange from one to the other as opposed to a naturally grounded claim to belonging in the political community. In this sense, we begin to see an unintended effect of Spanglish. Perhaps the very process of differentiation that one assumes to be the result of two preexisting language forms (that is, Spanglish as the privileged "third space") is, instead, that which allows us to understand such language forms as distinct markers of geopolitical origin *in the first place*. It is not so much about a subversive potential of mixture, in other words, as it is about the generation of difference itself. If Spanglish is the lingua franca—or if Spanglish were to stand in for any form of mixture such that one would never be able to trace language use to geopolitical location—then one might never be able to form political community around linguistic identity. Spanglish, in this sense, disallows one from determining whether language use signifies identity or difference—English or Spanish, alien or citizen—and traces a site of ambivalence, in formal terms, that subverts the certainty of both. Gómez-Peña never ascribes Spanglish to a specific location or subjectivity as identity or difference but, instead, marks it as an assumption for a politics of languaging in which origin, territory, and sovereign order are revealed to be built on nothing more than a historical fiction that *itself* produces difference.

As Homi Bhabha remarks, the procedure of hegemony is "quite literally, *unsignifiable* without the metonymic representation of its agonistic and ambivalent structure of articulation," for "the work of hegemony" is "itself the process of iteration and differentiation. It depends on the alternative or antagonistic images that are always produced side by side and in competition with each other."[51] Whereas hegemony operates by simultaneously constituting the inside/outside together and grounding "illegal" immigration exterior to the domain of law and thereby identifying the language that migrants are assumed to bring with them as beyond the domain of law, Gómez-Peña short-circuits the logic of difference itself and allows us to see its generation not in any natural fact (like an assumed geopolitical-linguistic difference) but through discourse itself.

If sovereignty is articulated in tandem with its exterior (non-West; colonial periphery) such that the exterior serves as the very interior condition of possibility, then what appears to cause the radical nativist's anxiety is a break in the relation between citizenship and language. When the radical nativist claims that "You people are determined to destroy our democracy, just because we give you the freedom to do it" and then refuses to engage Gómez-Peña when he responds in Spanglish, he inadvertently translates the difference between citizen and alien as indifferent to the law of the sovereign. The radical nativist inadvertently causes the occluded logic of the sovereign exception to momentarily appear, which articulates the indifference of the law itself to the difference between citizen and alien. That is, including the illegal alien in the situation ("we give you the freedom to do it") momentarily causes an excess of political community despite whatever particular laws or language practices regulate the terms for inclusion into the domain of citizen.

Gómez-Peña's response is therefore political in the sense that it effectively subverts the discursive economy of identity/difference, from the perspective of those who have no part. If the figure of the Spanish-speaking undocumented migrant represents the signifier that the "radical nativist" relies on to maintain the legitimacy of U.S.-American sovereignty, then the breakdown of this signifier into ambivalent indistinction collapses not only his assumptions of an uncontaminated national identity, existing separately from the illegal migrant, but, additionally, his foundational understanding of alien/native as the only choices for determining the conditions of belonging. The "radical nativist's" conception of juridical space—and of the registers of signification that correspond to such a distinction—simply do not map seamlessly onto the ruptured "foreign planet" that is neither Western nor non-Western but now something altogether different.

Such is the case of Gómez-Peña's identification of his interlocutor as a "radical nativist," which interrupts the discourse of indigeneity itself. Where one would normally expect to encounter the charge of nativism in a context of a Westerner who fetishizes indigeneity to the point of elevating it, Gómez-Peña's use of the term exposes the logic of the sovereign exception at work: by labeling what we can assume to be a "native speaking" U.S. citizen as a "radical nativist," he short-circuits this logic by drawing an indistinction between alien and native to the point that both begin to lose their value as a signifier of origin. Gómez-Peña offers a doubly opposite claim: this is not about who was in the territory of the United States first or about to whom this territory really belongs. It is not even about turning the logic of the state back on itself. Instead, the more radical claim at work here is Gómez-Peña's displacement of the economy of identity/difference that underwrites the oppositions of Spanish/English and alien/native.

When we speak of Latin America, or the U.S.-Mexico border that often serves as the topos for forms of rhetorical invention like "border thinking" or "mestiza rhetorics," as an object of analysis—when we reflect on Latin America with the goal of thinking how it could have always been, how it might yet still be and might have always been otherwise—we produce the very referent as a sign-effect of that which the sign "Latin America" is intended to refer. To speak of rhetoric or democracy in Latin America, still, will create an impossible task: it will require the analyst to read the text, whichever text, under the heading of an atopos: of a commonplace made uncommon but also of a proper name not yet sedimented. This undocumenting condition forecloses on the authority of any one rhetorical option; it is the space of a reading that remains undetermined; and it unconceals the possibility of a future that no knowledge machine could ever calculate and translate into civic administration.

Postscript | Rhetoric in the Non-name of All

There is no need to fear or hope, but only to look for new weapons.
—Gilles Deleuze, "Postscript on the Societies of Control"

This book opened with an attempt to analyze dominant rhetorics of undocumented immigration at the U.S.-Mexico border without submitting my analysis to their logics. I examined topoi of apprehension as sources of rhetorical invention in both Prevention Through Deterrence immigration policies and public arguments that sought to change Prevention Through Deterrence immigration policies. I also read apprehension as a commonplace (whose semantic range includes *to know*, *to capture*, and *to fear* others) informing practices of academic knowledge production, where the will to document undocumented migration, even from a place of counterhegemonic benevolence, comes with a will to capture. I tried to practice building knowledge grounded in something otherwise than the will to know by reading marks left behind by a fugitive and uncapturable rhetoricity I identified as rhetorical disinvention. Instead of attempting to apprehend representations of undocumented immigration, I examined disinventions that would foreclose on apprehending others and instead prompt regard for the responsibilities of addressing those who have yet to arrive.

I close this book by returning to a moment in 2014 that defined my research agenda and pushed me to begin thinking through a set of questions raised by María Lugones that, in my mind, remain relevant to rhetorical studies: "How do we learn about each other? How do we do it without harming each other but with the courage to take up a weaving of the everyday that may reveal deep betrayals? How do we cross over without taking over? With whom do we do this work?"[1] In these concluding pages, I return to that moment and offer some parting words in the form of a few concept metaphors for new lines of flight.

I feel hopeless in July 2014 when I see an Associated Press photograph of four women and their children in Border Patrol custody on the front page of *The Huffington Post*. Most of the subjects in the photograph are looking at something to the right, off camera. The women clutch the children, who in turn appear distressed. The title of the article reads, "U.S. Deports Honduran Children in First Flight Since Obama's Pledge." I feel hopeless because the image of the women and their children has become a floating, instrumentalized commonplace in public arguments about immigration. The same photograph is published in *The New York Times* and *The Christian Science Monitor* for different news stories.[2] The photograph that captures the suffering on the faces of women and child migrants, perhaps inviting viewers to "look cruelly," in Christa Olson's words,[3] would go on to instrumentalize their suffering in both benevolent attempts to humanize these people[4] and cruel rhetorics calling for an increase in the very immigration state apparatus that produces their suffering.[5]

None of it feels right. I had met two of the women and their children from the photograph a few weeks earlier on what I remember to be a very hot day in Tucson, Arizona. I was a volunteer at Casa Alitas, a humanitarian aid project of Catholic Community Services of Southern Arizona, with two colleagues from graduate school at the University of Arizona. Each afternoon around 4:00 p.m., an ICE van pulls into the driveway of Casa Alitas and unloads a group of undocumented migrants. Only women and children arrive in that van. Men and boys older than sixteen are taken, I'm told, to detention at a federal facility in Eloy, Arizona.

On this day, I convinced my partner to volunteer with me. She's worried she isn't up to the task because she doesn't speak Spanish. I remind her that some of the families don't speak Spanish either. Some speak Chuj or K'iche'. Besides, my Spanish isn't great either. What's important is that we're there, unconditionally, even beyond the possibility of understanding through communication. We're there to address whoever might arrive.

My partner and I spend the evening with the children from two families while the mothers rest in the air-conditioned house. We pile stones for makeshift goalposts and play soccer in the backyard. I suffer an embarrassing nutmeg, perhaps the premier dribbling skill in all of soccer, at the feet of one child. He seals my humiliation by blasting the ball across the goal line while I'm crumpled in defeat. There's no coming back from this, so I shout my best Andrés Cantor impression to ease the shame: "¡Goooooooool!"

I never ask the children, "Why did you come to the United States?" Does it matter anyway? Would I need that information to share in community with them? Do I need *a reason* to be hospitable?

We pick vegetables from the garden in the backyard as the sun disappears behind the Tucson Mountains west of town. I grew up in the Pacific Northwest, and I'm amazed at what will grow in the Arizona heat, given enough care and love. You see, the running joke is, "sure it's hot in Arizona, but it's a dry hate." Arizona SB 1070 and Arizona HB 2281 were both in effect in 2011 when Arizona State Senator Ron Gould sponsored Arizona SB 1309, a bill proposing to end birthright citizenship for U.S.-born children of undocumented migrants. And remember Maricopa County Sheriff Joe Arpaio? In 2007, Lou Dobbs asked Arpaio on CNN to respond to critics of his agency's tactics on illegal immigration enforcement. Arpaio responded, "Well, you know, they call you KKK. They did me. I think it's an honor, right? It means we're doing something."[6] He was the Maricopa County sheriff who forced incarcerated peoples to live in tent cities and wear pink (as though wearing pink is a punishment). He was the one who was found by a Department of Justice investigator in 2011 to have discriminated against Latinos in violation of the Constitution and the Civil Rights Act in "the most egregious racial profiling in the United States that he had ever personally observed in the course of his work."[7] Arpaio refused to comply with an order to direct the Maricopa County Sheriff's Office to end its practices of racial profiling.

At any rate, our job that day is to drive the families to their next destination after dark. My partner and I load the two families into the van: two women and their children, two women who, according to the law, don't have the right to sell their labor for a wage, even though plenty of businesses will still hire them; children who, according to the law, shouldn't qualify for basic social services. According to the law, they are entitled to no part and no place in U.S.-American civic space. It's as if they're *here*—materially countable under neoliberal logics via their labor productivity contributing to GDP— and at the same time they don't belong under civic logics. It's not exactly that they've been excluded from civic space but that their belonging to civic space is defined by not having a part in it.

I drive the van into the driveway of our next destination, and I mash the brake pedal because there are ten armed militiamen standing in a row blocking the driveway. They're preventing us from driving any further. I stop because they are armed with assault rifles. I panic. They are wearing bandoliers, kevlar vests, tactical boots, and face masks. One is holding an unsheathed bowie knife. I put the van in reverse and mash the gas pedal. We drive back to Casa Alitas.

What were they outfitted for, exactly, these militiamen? Had they anticipated a situation in which this kind of preparation would be necessary? And what were they prepared to do? Was this an intimidation tactic, a borderlands equivalent of a burning cross? And how did they know we would be there? How did they know we would be driving in that particular maroon van, on that night, at that time?

Useless

Disinventions takes off from motifs of fugitive and exorbitant semiosis I examined in this book (misapprehension, displacement, misunderstanding, misidentification, and undocumenting). I think a politics of disinvention would be useless, by which I mean, drawing from Jean-Luc Nancy, inoperative: unable to produce a practical use in the context of neoliberalism, where inquiry in the humanities often must justify itself by appealing to its instrumental usefulness.[8] I read disinvention in discourses of undocumented migrancy, which yield a weak force of demand for an incalculable (as opposed to a specific) configuration of civic life. It is in this sense of uselessness that I framed disinvention as an exorbitant and fugitive semiosis that "punches a hole" in the field of knowledge from which it emerges and draws limits on power/knowledge.[9]

At stake in my reading of disinvention is the prospect of building a knowledge that actively subverts itself. This is what I would be willing to call decolonization, which as I mentioned in chapter 2, produces an atopical, postidentitarian commitment to thought in what Acosta calls "the non-name of All," for if it were to be successful, it would displace its own grounding as commonplace in the process. As a resource for inventing arguments, decoloniality invents the necessity of its own displacement. The stakes, in other words, are the possibility for academic work to amount to something otherwise than an apprehension of difference. Excuse me for the clunky neologisms throughout the book, but political change requires changes in form. That said, what I'm proposing won't yield more university accounting or civic administration but could, perhaps, yield a knowledge that works to displace itself—a knowledge yielding a clearing for others to emerge beyond apprehension.

Emergent

There is precedent for this kind of useless or inoperative rhetoric. Jim Corder, for example, proposed to frame rhetoric around an impasse of rhetorical invention that arises in disputes. "Each of us is a narrative," Corder writes. We are assemblages of self-narrativizing matter: "We are always, as the rhetorician might say, inventing the narratives that are our lives."[10] Sometimes our narratives are congruent with others'. We might agree with someone else, from the perspective of our narrativized lived experience, that it is wrong to deport undocumented migrants. Sometimes our narratives are incongruent with others' but can be invented otherwise to become congruent. Sometimes, however, another narrative confronts our own, impossible to incorporate into our own without fundamentally threatening ours, perhaps reminding us that ours was invented through the unintelligibility of theirs. "When this happens," Corder says, "our narratives become indeed what they are perpetually becoming—arguments."[11] Therefore, we are arguments, too. But what happens when a situation becomes impassive, deadlocked to the degree that there is no language available, drawn from the right commonplace, spoken at the opportune moment, delivered in the right way, to change the other's mind? What could release us from the hopelessness of impassive, mutually exclusive arguments? Corder's answer is provisional: "If we are to hope for ourselves and to value all others, we must learn that argument is emergence [toward the other]."[12]

According to Corder, rhetoric does not have to presuppose that successful argument is possible, or perhaps even desirable, where successful means forcing a change of mind in an interlocutor. Where does the right to persuade come from anyway? What right do we have to expect another to acquiesce when we are perhaps that very incompatibility for the other? At what cost do we maintain our narrative? At what point does our own narrative become right supremacy?

In fact, and with sincere apologies to the New Rhetorics, I don't think rhetoric always has to be about identification. Instead, and recalling Spivak's definition from the introduction, rhetoric is "the name for the residue of indeterminacy which escapes the system . . . of what escapes even an exhaustive system of tro-pological analysis."[13] Rhetoric, in these terms, is a confrontation with right supremacy—with the presupposition that the right word with the right persua-sive power can be found *at all*. But argument, Corder says, "is not display or presentation," for when it is, it turns into the force of police.[14] Instead, if argu-ment begins in inventional impasse, in rhetorical disinvention, perhaps one might arrive at "the place where we are advocates of contending narratives (with their accompanying feelings and thoughts), where we are adversaries, each seeming to propose the repudiation or annihilation of what the other lives, val-ues, and is, where we are beyond being adversaries in that strange kind of argu-ment we seldom attend to, where one offers the other a rightness so demanding, a beauty so stunning, a grace so fearful as to call the hearer to forego one iden-tity for a startling new one."[15] Rhetoric, if it is to be about preparing oneself to perceive not just one normative group but any group, then it means that before we listen we have to first take the impassive disposition of being ready to hear anyone at all, which also means no one in particular. The speaker of the mes-sage might be someone of whom you are a formal representative; but they also might be someone whom you don't formally represent, and you might become an informal representative of someone beyond your choosing to do so. You might get hailed into becoming an informal representative of someone com-pletely foreign.

It is neither possible nor desirable to only prepare ourselves to receive the speech of those whom we formally represent anyway. Where could one think from to avoid reproducing the thorny problem of speaking for others? Alcoff argues that "if a privileging of the oppressed's speech cannot be made on the grounds that its content will necessarily be liberatory, it can be made on the grounds of the very act of speaking. Speaking constitutes a subject that chal-lenges and subverts the opposition between the knowing agent and the object of knowledge, an opposition that is key in the reproduction of imperialist modes of discourse. The problem with speaking for others exists in the very structure of discursive practice, no matter its content, and therefore it is this structure itself that needs alteration."[16] Alcoff reframes the question of speaking for oth-ers within the category of speech itself, not merely its effects. The problem of speaking for others is not an effect of speech, a misrepresentation of an other, such that one could go and find the correct words that would be perfectly corre-spondent to an other. The last sentence is important: the problem exists in the structure of discursive practice—no matter its content. The problem of speaking for others is structural, meaning that it is not subject to change by finding the right words to objectively present the voice of others.

My project can't locate an authentic speaker or listener as its representative. However, it does investigate how the speaker/listener structure requires an informal, perhaps even postidentitarian disposition. Spivak, for example, writes,

> The question of "speaking as" involves a distancing from oneself. The moment I have to think of the ways in which I will speak as an Indian, or as a feminist, the ways in which I will speak as a woman, what I am trying to do is generalise myself, make myself a representative, trying to distance myself from some kind of inchoate speaking *as such*. . . . But when the cardcarrying listeners, the hegemonic people, the dominant people, talk about listening to someone "speaking as" something or the other, I think *there* one encounters a problem. When *they* want to hear an Indian speaking as an Indian, a Third World woman speaking as a Third World woman, they cover over the fact of the ignorance that they are allowed to possess, into a kind of homogenization.[17]

While Spivak is not strictly commenting on the question of speaking for others, she notes how the event of speaking as other is already structured by a listener's desire to hear her "speaking as" and can overdetermine the content of her speech. Even speaking for oneself requires one to generalize oneself as a representative of oneself. In remaining nonspecific, or informal, rhetorical theory can open clearings for questions about "how to develop strategies for a more equitable, just distribution of the ability to speak and be heard."[18]

Hospitable

Speaking of the emergence of others, over the past ten years, we have witnessed emergent forms of migration with, for example, a surge of unaccompanied child migrants in 2014 and the more recent migrant caravans from the Central American Northern Triangle. The root causes of these recent waves of migration from Central American nations are heterogeneous, as seismic cultural, economic, and political shifts have resulted from Latin America's turbulent transition to late capitalism over the past century.[19] However, there is no debate that anthropogenic climate change has caused drought and crop failure, exacerbating forms of political destabilization that have been ongoing for more than fifty years. And while these recent waves have brought hundreds and thousands of migrants at a time, it is reasonable to believe that, given current climate models and predictions, in the near future we will see perhaps tens of thousands of undocumented migrants per wave. Our current models of political community grounded in citizenship—and our current theories of political resistance premised as they are in decolonizing the U.S.-Mexico borderlands—are simply inadequate to lend explanatory power to the magnitude of migration that is sure to arrive. My wager in this book is that a different mode of political thought is possible, one premised in a kind of postidentitarian hospitality unmoored from the metaphysics of the subject that requires people to be known as the condition of possibility to be accepted into a community.

The question of hospitality toward undocumented migrants is simple: as I see it, violent policies and practices of immigration enforcement must be abolished, and undocumented migrants should be welcomed without conditions. The question of hospitality is also not simple, for as Derrida observed, there is an impasse structuring the logic of hospitality: to let the stranger in, the host must first hold the authority to close the stranger out. In other words, if critics are to argue that migrants should be welcomed, then we make that argument knowing that it will be authorized by the imperium of the settler colonial nation-state. The question *of* hospitality, the question of "what arrives at the borders," is a question of how to respond to the stranger who arrives at the doorstep of the dwelling. To be hospitable to the stranger, however, requires a host to enter into an impasse: "How can we distinguish between a guest and a parasite? In principle, the difference is straightforward, but for that you need a law; hospitality, reception, the welcome offered, have to be submitted to a basic and limiting jurisdiction."[20] The logic of hospitality requires that if a host is to be hospitable, to be welcoming and inclusive, a host must initially be closed off and exclusive. To be welcomed in, a stranger must first be marked as a foreigner—the law of hospitality presupposes and constitutes the stranger as its primary condition of possibility. And yet, "in order to constitute the space of a habitable house and a home, you have to give up a passage to the outside world [*l'etranger*]. There is no house or interior without a door or windows."[21] We might reguard the stranger, guard an unconditional openness toward the stranger, as a primary rhetoricity. If the law of hospitality first requires a host to be inhospitable, then it also requires a host to remain impossibly open to whomever, whatsoever. There can be no interior (no community) without an opening (a window or a door)—an opening that writes no law about who may enter but merely remains open toward the stranger yet to arrive.

A rhetoric of migrant hospitality does not have to be about persuasion: speaking the proper words or listening to the right people or even having the word at all. It can be about rejecting the desire, or requirement, to know someone as the grounds to have something in common with them. Rhetorical inquiry can be structured on developing shared values beyond the will to know: on preparing oneself to be open to perceive on the basis of not knowing; of not needing to know someone as the condition of possibility for relating; of clearing the grounds, so to speak, for someone else to show up on their own terms. If we set prior conditions out before listening, for example, we foreclose on the arrival of the other. Hospitality, on the other hand, is about receiving someone whom we do not know on their terms.

Dangerous

I understand that asking readers to consider unconditional hospitality is a huge ask on any reader. It requires one to unlearn the logic of stranger danger that probably kept many of us safe as children. But I think stranger danger can also be a resource. Rhetorical studies can and should unlearn its commitments to exceptionalism that perhaps were once necessary but now complicate the collective project of pursuing what Kimberlé Williams Crenshaw calls "political intersectionality," as a means to "better acknowledge and ground the differences among us and negotiate the means by which these differences will find expression in constructing group politics."[22] There is more work to be done than simply registering examples of cultural production and arguing that an example expands the scope of what counts in the official archive of power/knowledge. I am not suggesting that kind of scholarship isn't valuable, of course. But perhaps more work can be done to account for the unintended effects of *any* articulation of ethnic exceptionalism. I think rhetorical studies can learn a great deal about the productions of differential identities from within Latinidad and Latinamericanism from scholars like Maylei Blackwell, Maritza Cárdenas, Lorgia García Peña, Renee Hudson, and María Josefina Saldaña-Portillo, whose ideas inspire me to pursue a rhetorical studies that would pose a danger to power/knowledge, anchored in the promise of ever more capacious and just futures for everyone, "in the non-name of All."

Notes

Introduction

1. I want to thank Romeo García, who assisted me on a research trip to Nogales, Sonora, Mexico, in the summer of 2018 to photograph this mural.
2. Acosta, *Thresholds of Illiteracy*, 237.
3. By "postnational," I refer not to the waning of the nation-state but its shift in post–Cold War times with the proliferation of nonnational formations (the Maastricht Treaty in Europe and the rise of paramilitary groups in the United States, Mexico, and Colombia), postnational flows of capital (NAFTA and CAFTA), and the exhaustion of previously functional models of nation-state hegemony across the entire Américan hemisphere. Brown, *Walled States, Waning Sovereignty*; Williams, *Other Side of the Popular*; Williams, *Infrapolitical Passages*.
4. Cacho, *Social Death*.
5. Masuoka and Junn, *Politics of Belonging*.
6. Rancière, *Disagreement*, 24–29.
7. Davis, *Inessential Solidarity*, 73.
8. Ballif, "Regarding the Dead," 455.
9. United States Customs and Border Protection, "U.S. Border Patrol Fiscal Year."
10. No More Deaths and La Coalición de Derechos Humanos, *Disappeared Report*, 5.
11. International Organization for Migration, "US-Mexico Border."
12. ABC News, "14 Illegal Immigrants Die"; Sterngold, "Devastating Picture."
13. Urrea, *Devil's Highway*, 108.
14. Béjar Lara, "Narrating Cross-Border Migration," 182.
15. Béjar Lara, "Narrating Cross-Border Migration," 179.
16. Urrea, *Devil's Highway*, 71–72.
17. Foucault, *Lectures on the Will to Know*, 217.
18. Graff Zivin, *Anarchaeologies*, 144.
19. Guha, "Prose of Counter-Insurgency."
20. Spivak, "Deconstructing Historiography," 16.
21. Negri, "Twenty Theses on Marx," 159.
22. Žižek, "From Politics to Biopolitics," 395.
23. Moreiras, *Exhaustion of Difference*, 18
24. Derrida, *Rogues*, 148–59.
25. Cf. Makoni and Pennycook, "Disinventing and (Re)Constituting Languages." I draw the concept of disinvention from the linguists Sinfree Makoni and Alastair Pennycook, who argue that critics constitute their objects of analysis through the prism of prior "metadiscursive regimes" of knowledge.
26. Foucault, *Lectures on the Will to Know*, 217.
27. My use of "emergent property" comes from Manuel DeLanda's theory of assemblages. See DeLanda, *New Philosophy of Society*, 10.
28. Muñoz, *Disidentifications*, 179, 176.
29. Spivak, Sipiora, and Atwill, "Rhetoric and Cultural Explanation," 29.

30. Rancière, *Disagreement*, 30.
31. Rancière, *Disagreement*, 28.
32. Rancière, *Disagreement*, 29.
33. For more information on the concept of topos in rhetorical studies, refer to Benson, "Senses of Rhetoric"; Chirindo, "Rhetorical Places"; Consigny, "Rhetoric and Its Situations"; Eide, "Aristotelian Topos and Greek Geometry"; Leff, "Up from Theory"; McKeon, "Creativity and the Commonplace"; Miller, "Aristotle's 'Special Topics'"; Wallace, "Topoi and the Problem of Invention."
34. Olson, *Constitutive Visions*, 5–6.
35. Cintrón, "Democracy and its Limitations," 100.
36. Kennerly, "Atopia"; Reeves, "Suspended Identification"; Vitanza, *Negation*, 62–68.
37. Kennerly, "Atopia," 54–55.
38. Foucault, *Order of Things*, xix.
39. Derrida, *Rogues*, xiv.
40. Derrida, *Rogues*, xv.
41. Foucault, *Lectures on the Will to Know*, 217.
42. Chávez, *Queer Migrations*; Saldaña-Portillo, "Violence of Citizenship."
43. Derrida, *Rogues*, 149.
44. Scott, *Domination and the Arts of Resistance*, 183.
45. Bennington, *Scatter 1*.
46. Badiou, *Ethics*, 70.
47. Moreiras, *Exhaustion of Difference*, 96.
48. De León, *Land of Open Graves*, 9.
49. Aldama, *Disrupting Savagism*; Brady, *Extinct Lands, Temporal Geographies*; Calderón and Saldívar, *Criticism in the Borderlands*; Castillo and Tabuenca Córdoba, *Border Women*; Chávez, *Queer Migrations*; Cisneros, *Border Crossed Us*; Guidotti-Hernández, *Unspeakable Violence*; Guzmán, *Universal Citizenship*; Hartelius, *Rhetorics of US Immigration*; Hernández, *Bad Mexicans*; Lugones, *Pilgrimages/Peregrinajes*; Ramírez, *Occupying Our Space*; Ribero, *Dreamer Nation*; Saldaña-Portillo, *Indian Given*; Saldívar, *Border Matters*; Walker, *Climate Politics on the Border*.
50. DeChaine, *Border Rhetorics*; Chávez, "Border (In)Securities"; Chávez, "Embodied Translation"; Calafell, "Disrupting the Dichotomy"; Flores, "Constructing Rhetorical Borders"; Lechuga and De La Garza, "Forum: Border Rhetorics"; Maldonado, "Rhetorical Rumors"; Ono and Sloop, *Shifting Borders*; Sowards, *Rhetoricity of Borders*.
51. Flores, *Deportable and Disposable*.
52. DeChaine, "Introduction," 9.
53. Dussel, "Eurocentrism and Modernity," 65.
54. Graff Zivin, *Anarchaeologies*, 34.
55. Hatfield, *Limits of Identity*, 3.
56. Moreiras, *Exhaustion of Difference*, 127.
57. García and Cortez, "Trace of a Mark That Scatters"; Cortez and García, "Absolute Limit of Latinx Writing."
58. Bhabha, *Location of Culture*, 37.
59. Spivak, "Can the Subaltern Speak?," 271.
60. Acosta, *Thresholds of Illiteracy*, 6.
61. Derrida, *Of Grammatology*, 20.
62. Spivak, "Can the Subaltern Speak?," 285.
63. Spivak, "Deconstructing Historiography," 11.
64. Spivak, "Deconstructing Historiography," 13.

65. Spivak, "Can the Subaltern Speak?," 286.

66. Cf. Deleuze, *Difference and Repetition*, especially chapter 5, "Asymmetrical Synthesis of the Sensible," for his discussion of "intensive qualities."

67. Lyotard, *Differend*; Rancière, *Disagreement*, 22.

68. Anzaldúa, *Borderlands*; Baca, *Mestiz@ Scripts*; Flores and Benmayor, *Latino Cultural Citizenship*; Rosaldo, *Culture and Truth*; García Canclini, *Consumers and Citizens*; Saldívar, *Border Matters*; Stavans, *Hispanic Condition*; Taylor-García, *Existence of the Mixed Race Damnés*.

69. DeChaine, "Introduction," 5.

70. Carrera, *Imagining Identity in New Spain*; Katzew, *Casta Painting*; Martínez, *Genealogical Fictions*.

71. Foucault writes that power is never given at the outset in any context but rather is immanent to the mechanisms of its contexts, which "makes it possible to use its mechanisms as a grid of intelligibility of the social order." Foucault, *History of Sexuality, Volume 1*, 93.

72. Acosta, *Thresholds of Illiteracy*, 241

73. Moreiras, *Exhaustion of Difference*, 32.

Chapter 1

1. Boyce, Chambers, and Launius, "Bodily Inertia"; Cantú, *Line Becomes a River*; Cornelius, "Death at the Border"; Hing, *American Presidents*; De Genova, "Anonymous Brown Bodies"; De León, *Land of Open Graves*; Doty, "Bare Life"; Dunn, *Blockading the Border and Human Rights*; Massey, Pren, and Durand, "Why Border Enforcement Backfired"; Fernandez, "Path to America"; María García, *Seeking Refuge*; Massey and Pren, "Unintended Consequences"; Marquez, "Latinos as the 'Living Dead'"; Martínez et al., "Structural Violence"; Nevins, *Operation Gatekeeper*; Rosas, "Managed Violences of the Borderlands"; Stephen, "*Los nuevos desaparecidos*"; Traux, *We Built the Wall*.

2. Farrell, "Weight of Rhetoric," 470.

3. United States Customs and Border Protection, "Nationwide Enforcement Encounters."

4. Brady, *Extinct Lands, Temporal Geographies*, 13, 18.

5. St. John, *Line in the Sand*.

6. Parra, "Valientes Nogalenses," 20.

7. St. John, "Raging Controversy."

8. Lim, *Porous Borders*, 54

9. Ettinger, "'We Sometimes Wonder What They Will Spring on Us Next,'" 180–81.

10. Chavez, *Latino Threat*; Gutiérrez, *Walls and Mirrors*.

11. Flores, *Deportable and Disposable*, 4.

12. Ngai, "Strange Career of the Illegal Alien," 85.

13. Molina, *How Race Is Made in America*.

14. Hernández, *Migra!*

15. Camacho, *Migrant Imaginaries*; Swords and Mize, *Consuming Mexican Labor*.

16. Massey and Pren, "Unintended Consequences"; Ngai, "Strange Career of the Illegal Alien."

17. Clinton, "Remarks," 1194.

18. Ekstrand, *Border Control*, 3.

19. Sandia National Laboratories, *Systematic Analysis*, ES-4.

20. Sandia National Laboratories, *Systematic Analysis*, ES-5.

21. Sandia National Laboratories, *Systematic Analysis*, 7.

22. Sandia National Laboratories, *Systematic Analysis*, 143.

23. Sandia National Laboratories, *Systematic Analysis*, 201.

24. United States Border Patrol, *Border Patrol Strategic Plan*, 1.

25. United States Border Patrol, *Border Patrol Strategic Plan*, 6.

26. United States Border Patrol, *Border Patrol Strategic Plan*, 6 (emphasis added).

27. United States Immigration and Naturalization Service, *Building a Comprehensive Southwest Border Enforcement Strategy*, 3.

28. Stana, *Illegal Immigration*, 27.

29. *Guardian*, "Kamala Harris Tells Migrants."

30. Mukasey and Chertoff, "Transcript."

31. United States House of Representatives, *Providing for Consideration of H.R. 6061* (statement of Ed Royce).

32. Mukasey and Chertoff, "Transcript."

33. Martin, "How 1994's Operation Gatekeeper."

34. Martin, "How 1994's Operation Gatekeeper."

35. Martin, "How 1994's Operation Gatekeeper."

36. Massey, "Borderline Madness," 137.

37. Meissner and Kerwin, *DHS and Immigration: Taking Stock and Correcting Course*, 14–15.

38. Agamben, *Homo Sacer*, 1.

39. Agamben, *Homo Sacer*, 9.

40. By "spatial crisis," I reference the form of power that Gilles Deleuze calls "control" ("Postscript on the Societies of Control," 4).

41. Cacho, *Social Death*.

42. Appadurai, *Modernity at Large*; Augé, *Non-places*.

43. Fan, "When Deterrence and Death Mitigation Fall Short," 725.

44. Allyn and Marizco, "Jury Acquits Aid Worker."

45. Zhao et al., "Global Patterns."

46. T. Miller, *Border Patrol Nation*, 60.

47. Wong, *Politics of Immigration*, 60.

48. Martínez et al., *Migrant Deaths in Southern Arizona*, 15.

49. No More Deaths and La Coalición de Derechos Humanos, *Disappeared Report*, 7.

50. O'Dell, González, and Castellano, "'Mass Disaster' Grows."

51. Fisher, "Don't Force Me to Mourn."

52. Corradini et al., *Operation Streamline*, 1.

53. Derrida, *Rogues*, xi.

54. Derrida, *Rogues*, xiv.

55. Derrida, *Rogues*, xv.

Chapter 2

1. Mignolo, *Darker Side of the Renaissance*, vii.

2. Mignolo, "Geopolitics of Knowledge," 66.

3. Baca, "Rethinking Composition," 229.

4. Baca, *Mestiz@ Scripts*, 31.

5. Wanzer-Serrano, "Decolonial Rhetoric," 327–28.

6. Romney, "Rhetoric from the Margins," 238, 247.

7. Olson, "Places to Stand," 79.

8. See, for example, Agnew et al., "Octalog III"; Mao, "Doing Comparative Rhetoric Responsibly"; Mao et al., "Manifesting a Future for Comparative Rhetoric"; Shome, "Postcolonial Interventions"; Stroud, "Pragmatism."

9. Williams, *Other Side of the Popular*, 78–89.

10. Latin American Subaltern Studies Group, "Founding Statement," 110.

11. Murphy et al., "Politics of Historiography," 5.

12. Murphy et al., "Politics of Historiography," 12.

13. Alcoff, "Problem of Speaking for Others," 7.

14. Alcoff, "Problem of Speaking for Others," 7.

15. Alcoff, "Problem of Speaking for Others," 7.

16. Cf. Ratcliffe, *Rhetorical Listening*.

17. Murphy et al., "Politics of Historiography," 5.

18. Dussel, "Eurocentrism and Modernity," 65.

19. Mignolo, *Darker Side of the Renaissance*, 455.

20. Beasley-Murray, *Posthegemony*, 4.

21. Mignolo, "Colonial and Postcolonial Discourse," 130 (emphasis mine).

22. Mignolo, *Darker Side of the Renaissance*, 331–32.

23. For more on the discourse of exceptionalism, see Rodríguez Matos, "After the Ruin of Thinking"; Lund, "Barbarian Theorizing."

24. Mignolo, *Darker Side of the Renaissance*, xii.

25. Mignolo, "Geopolitics of Knowledge," 91 (emphasis mine).

26. By "exception," I refer to what Joshua Lund describes as a tendency to value Latin American ideas over non–Latin American ideas on the grounds that the former is a space where ideologically universal theories of society both meet their end (do not belong) and fail to be produced (do not emerge). Lund, "Barbarian Theorizing," 55.

27. Baca, preface to *Rhetorics of the Americas*, ix.

28. Baca, preface to *Rhetorics of the Americas*, ix.

29. Baca, "Te-Ixtli," 3.

30. Ramírez, *Occupying Our Space*, 14.

31. Ramírez, *Occupying Our Space*, 21, 52, 49.

32. Ramírez, *Occupying Our Space*, 50.

33. Mignolo, "Geopolitics of Knowledge," 66. Further, from the vantage of decoloniality, exemplified by the "four horses of the apocalypse," Western philosophy is understood to be *inherently* flawed. See Grosfoguel, "Decolonizing Post-Colonial Studies"; Mallon, "Promise and Dilemma of Subaltern Studies"; Rodríguez, "Reading Subalterns."

34. Mignolo and Tlostanova, "Theorizing from the Borders," 206.

35. Mignolo, "Delinking."

36. Grosfoguel, "Decolonizing Post-Colonial Studies."

37. Cisneros, *Border Crossed Us*.

38. Baca, *Mestiz@ Scripts*; Lunsford, "Toward a Mestiza Rhetoric"; Ramírez, *Occupying Our Space*.

39. Moreiras, *Exhaustion of Difference*, 6.

40. Moreiras, *Exhaustion of Difference*, 277.

41. Acosta, *Thresholds of Illiteracy*, 73.

42. Acosta, *Thresholds of Illiteracy*, 73.

43. Graff Zivin, *Anarchaeologies*, 13.

44. Murphy et al., "Politics of Historiography," 5.

45. Burke, *Attitudes Toward History*, 173

46. Vitanza, "After/word," 237.

47. Hatfield, *Limits of Identity*, 48.

48. Williams, *Other Side of the Popular*, 35.

49. Williams, *Other Side of the Popular*, 280.

Chapter 3

1. I use quotation marks around the signs "alien" and "illegal immigrant" because I want to read the language used by the legislation while signaling to readers that I condemn grammars of white supremacy.

2. Archibold, "Arizona Enacts Stringent Law."

3. Brewer, "Arizona Gov. Jan Brewer Explains."

4. Although the bill was the first of its kind to be signed into law, similar bills were introduced in Arizona, Texas, Colorado, and California before Arizona SB 1070. Cf. M. T. García, *Desert Immigrants*; Guidotti-Hernández, *Unspeakable Violence*; Lim, *Porous Borders*; Ono and Sloop, *Shifting Borders*.

5. There can be no doubt, of course, about the violence and impunity that Mexican and Mexican Americans will have faced at the hands of the U.S.-American state. Nevertheless, the persistent framing of migrants as Mexican—and of the ethos of migrancy in the space of the U.S.-Mexico border in general as a Mexican—suggests how border space itself has always already been racialized as either Anglo or Mexican/Mexican American to the point that other ethnic minorities are rendered differently intelligible.

6. Olson and de los Santos, "Expanding the Idea of America," 197.

7. Cf. Bokser, "Sor Juana's Rhetoric of Silence"; Bokser, "Reading and Writing Sor Juana's Arch"; Calafell, "Disrupting the Dichotomy"; Cisneros, *Border Crossed Us*; Enoch, "Survival Stories"; Izaguirre, "'Social Movement in Fact'"; Medina, *Reclaiming Poch@ Pop*; Romney, "Indian Ability."

8. I borrow the phrase "inclusive exclusion" from Giorgio Agamben, who, in *Homo Sacer: Sovereign Power and Bare Life*, describes an element included in the structure of sovereignty via its exclusion from it.

9. Cf. Martínez, *Genealogical Fictions*. As Martínez has argued, the *sistema de castas* was influenced in part by the Spanish discourse of *limpieza de sangre*, which marked to the condition of having a clean Christian genealogy—that is, clean from Jewish or Muslim ancestry. Given that the purity of blood statutes (which were passed in Toledo, Spain, in 1449) were waged against converts (Jewish and Muslim *conversos*) to Christianity in Spain and that such statutes came into use in the colonial categories of *limpieza de sangre* in New Spain in the sixteenth century (specifically, as a means of maintaining colonial institutions like the Franciscan Order, for example), Martínez suggests that the entire tradition of racial formation in Latin America can be attributed, in part at least, to the perfection of the ideology of race on the Iberian Peninsula. How this discourse of faith became a discourse of blood, however, is still up for debate.

10. Cf. Esteva-Fabregat, *Mestizaje in Ibero-America*; Carrera, *Imagining Identity in New Spain*; Cope, *Limits of Racial Domination*; Katzew, *Casta Painting*.

11. Hernández Cuevas, "Mexican Colonial Term," 125.

12. Chandler, *X*, 101–2.

13. Derrida, *Truth in Painting*, 53, 59–60.

14. Derrida, *Truth in Painting*, 9.

15. Esteva-Fabregat, *Mestizaje in Ibero-America*, 78.

16. Vasconcelos, *Cosmic Race*, 32.

17. Horne, "Open Letter."

18. See Ore, *Lynching*, 19–22.

19. Ochoa O'Leary et al., "Assault on Ethnic Studies," 110.

20. Diaz, "I Am a Book Trafficker."

21. Modern Language Association, "Statement."

22. I ask the reader to refer to Dr. Ore's full account of her arrest, in her own words, "They Call Me Dr. Ore."

23. Ore, "They Call Me Dr. Ore."

24. Ore, "They Call Me Dr. Ore."

25. Rancière, *Disagreement*, 15.

26. Rancière, *Disagreement*, 4.

Chapter 4

1. Legal Information Institute, "8 U.S. Code § 1325."

2. I refer in shorthand to Sessions's policy as "zero tolerance." United States Department of Justice Office of Public Affairs, "Attorney General Announces Zero-Tolerance Policy."

3. Goodwin, *Immigration Enforcement*, 7.

4. Bump, "Here Are the Administration Officials"; Planas, "Trump's Family Separation Policy."

5. Hunter, "Long History of Child Snatching"; Miroff and Horwitz, "Trump Didn't Invent Family Separation."

6. United States Office of the Inspector General, *Review of the Department of Justice's Planning and Implementation*, 15.

7. Jordan, "I Have No Idea"; Jordan, "Family Members Separated at Border."

8. Dickerson, "Parents of 545 Children."

9. Shakira, "Parents of 545 Children."

10. Shakira, "Parents of 545 Children."

11. Shakira, "Parents of 545 Children."

12. Burke, *Language as Symbolic Action*, 45.

13. Chávez and Masri, "Rhetoric of Family in the U.S. Immigration Movement," 210.

14. Maldonado, "Manifestx," 106.

15. Flores, "Stoppage," 254.

16. Acosta, *Thresholds of Illiteracy*, 241.

17. Trump White House Archived, "06/26/19."

18. I choose not to include the photograph in this book because I argue that there is no reasoning, practical or otherwise, to be drawn from this photograph. What can be drawn from the photo is both excessive and immanent to reason: a misunderstanding, through which reasoning seizes up and through which an address toward the other without predicate is produced. I argue against the instrumentalization of such images of migrant death, even toward the ends of transforming federal immigration policy. I assume that readers have access to the search engine of their choice, where they can view the image if they choose.

19. Acosta, *Thresholds of Illiteracy*, 243.

20. Cf. Burke, *Rhetoric of Motives*, 41; Christensen, *Notes Toward a New Rhetoric*, 39.

21. Weingarten, "To All Parents."

22. Julian Castro (@JulianCastro), "Oscar and Valeria Martinez died on these shores—desperately crossing the river as a last resort for asylum. They aren't the first to be killed by Trump's immigration agenda, and they won't be the last if we don't act soon," *Twitter*, October 7, 2019, 8:44 a.m., https://twitter.com/juliancastro/status/1181233727025958918?lang=en.

23. Fredrick, "'Metering' at the Border."

24. Fleischer, "On Fox."

25. Kelly, Shoichet, and Alvarez, "Ken Cuccinelli Blames Drowned Man."

26. Kelly, Shoichet, and Alvarez, "Ken Cuccinelli Blames Drowned Man."

27. Trump White House Archived, "06/26/19."

28. RAICES, "We will not be sharing the graphic image published by AP of Óscar Alberto Martinez Ramírez and his 23-month old daughter, Valeria who drowned trying to cross the Rio Grande on Monday," Facebook, June 26, 2019, https://www.facebook.com/raicestexas/photos/a.10152272455314678/10156845775604678/?type=3.

29. Ahmed and Semple, "Photo of Drowned Migrants"; Takenaga, "Why the Times Published a Photo."

30. Cole, "Crime Scene at the Border."

31. Ahmed and Semple, "Photo of Drowned Migrants."

32. Barnard and Shoumali, "Image of Drowned Syrian."

33. Žižek and Dillworth, "Interview with Slavoj Zizek."

34. Rancière, *Disagreement*, xi.

35. Rancière, *Disagreement*, 30.

36. Žižek, *In Defense of Lost Causes*, 413.

37. Shakira, "Parents of 545 Children." *Comunidad malentendido* is a neologism, referring to both a communal misunderstanding about migration and a misunderstood community of undocumented migrants.

38. Legal Information Institute, "6 U.S. Code § 279."

39. United States Customs and Border Protection, "Southwest Land Border Encounters."

40. Luiselli, *Tell Me How It Ends*, 7.

41. Lyotard, *Differend*, 9.

42. I borrow and translate the phrase "the lost children" from Luiselli to refer to those whom the U.S. federal government calls "unaccompanied minor children." Luiselli's book was originally written in Spanish and published under the title *Los niños perdidos: Un ensayo en cuarenta preguntas*.

43. Kennerly, "Atopia," 54.

44. Luiselli, *Tell Me How It Ends*, 69.

Chapter 5

1. Pérez, *Decolonial Imaginary*, 11.

2. Pérez, *Decolonial Imaginary*, 11.

3. Pérez, *Decolonial Imaginary*, xvi–xvii.

4. Bhabha, *Location of Culture*, 122–23.

5. Pérez, *Decolonial Imaginary*, xii.

6. Pérez, *Decolonial Imaginary*, 5.

7. Ratcliffe, *Rhetorical Listening*, 17.

8. Ratcliffe, *Rhetorical Listening*, 25.

9. Ratcliffe, *Rhetorical Listening*, 20.

10. Ratcliffe, *Rhetorical Listening*, 76.

11. Ratcliffe, *Rhetorical Listening*, 27.

12. Ratcliffe, *Rhetorical Listening*, 46.

13. Ratcliffe, *Rhetorical Listening*, 24.

14. Graff Zivin, *Anarchaeologies*, 144.

15. Derrida, *Of Grammatology*, 70–71.

16. Moreiras, *Exhaustion of Difference*, 32.

17. Pérez, *Decolonial Imaginary*, 25.

18. Pérez, *Decolonial Imaginary*, 25.

19. Pérez, *Decolonial Imaginary*, 26.

20. Anzaldúa, *Borderlands*, 99.

21. Anzaldúa, *Borderlands*, 101–2.

22. Anzaldúa, *Borderlands*, 84.

23. Anzaldúa, *Borderlands*, 33, 113.

24. Williams, *Other Side of the Popular*, 30–31.

25. Williams, *Other Side of the Popular*, 31.

26. *The Decolonial Imaginary* emerged in close proximity to several other projects across Latino and Latin American cultural studies at the turn of the twenty-first century that reimagined the role of critical thought in relation to fundamental shifts in contemporary social, political, and scholarly formations in the wake of free-trade global capital, including Aparicio and Chávez, *Tropicalizations*; Beverley, *Subalternity and Representation*; Saldívar, *Border Matters*; Mignolo, *Local Histories/Global Designs*, Moreiras, *Exhaustion of Difference*; Poblete, *Critical Latin American and Latino Studies*; Sandoval, *Methodology of the Oppressed*; Williams, *Other Side of the Popular*.

27. Moreiras, *Exhaustion of Difference*, 20.

28. Moreiras, *Exhaustion of Difference*, 107.

29. Jacques Rancière argues that "politics exists simply because no social order is based on nature, no divine law regulates human society" (*Disagreement*, 16). If "sheer contingency," or a lack of grounding in divine law, is the first and primary condition of possibility for any social order, hegemony is the name for a rhetorical power of managing subjectivities, or "parts," proper to their place in society and of circulating "the lie that invents some kind of social nature in order to provide community with an *arkhē*" (Rancière, *Disagreement*, 16).

30. Williams, *Other Side of the Popular*, 1, 8.

31. Yúdice, "Civil Society," 4.

32. Hardt, "Withering of Civil Society," 40.

33. Gramsci, *Selections from the Prison Notebooks*, 238.

34. Cf. Deleuze, "Postscript on the Societies of Control."

35. Williams, *Other Side of the Popular*, 149.

36. Ballif, "Regarding the Dead"; Graff Zivin, *Anarchaeologies*, 30; Morieras, *Exhaustion of Difference*, 46.

37. Baca, *Mestiz@ Scripts*, 64.

38. Wolford, "Afterword," 278.

39. Howes, "Imagining a Multiplicity."

40. Austin and Montiel, "Codex Espangliensis," 99.

41. Medina, *Reclaiming Poch@ Pop*, 123.

42. Gómez-Peña, Chagoya, and Rice, *Codex Espangliensis*, screen 14/2.

43. Rancière *Disagreement*, 30.

44. Mendieta and Gómez-Peña, "Latino Philosopher," 549.

45. Žižek, *Puppet and the Dwarf*, 96.

46. Denarrativization, as Moreiras writes, names "the moment when a narrative, any narrative, breaks into its own abyss" and "a moment of flight in which subjectivity registers as noncapturable; indeed, it is a moment of pure production without positivity that will not let itself be exhaustively defined in the name of any heterogeneity" (*Exhaustion of Difference*, 56).

47. Žižek, *Puppet and the Dwarf*, 413.

48. Rice et al., *Documentado/Undocumented*, 68–69. The full text of this piece can also be accessed at https://docundoc.com/2005/07/24/we-are-here-because-you-are-there/.

49. Cf. Butler and Spivak, *Who Sings the Nation-State?*

50. Flores and Rosa, "Undoing Appropriateness."

51. Bhabha, *Location of Culture*, 44, 42.

Postscript

1. Lugones, "Toward a Decolonial Feminism," 755.

2. Hulse, "Immigrant Surge"; Fieser, "What Do 'Social Inclusion' Rankings Tell Us?"

3. Olson, "Cruel Looking."

4. Watts, "Driven by Fear."

5. Perry, "What Obama Missed on the Border"; Roberts, "Here's How GOP Can Get Back at Obama."

6. See TheMexicaMovement, "Sheriff Joe Arpaio Says It's an HONOR to Be Compared to KKK," YouTube, November 17, 2007, https://www.youtube.com/watch?v=VFTUQ71Aq00.

7. Johnson, "Probe Finds Arizona Sheriff Violated Civil Rights."

8. Nancy, *Inoperative Community*.

9. Badiou, *Ethics*, 70.

10. Corder, "Argument as Emergence," 16–17.

11. Corder, "Argument as Emergence," 18.

12. Corder, "Argument as Emergence," 26.

13. Spivak, Sipiora, and Atwill, "Rhetoric and Cultural Explanation," 294.

14. Corder, "Argument as Emergence," 26.

15. Corder, "Argument as Emergence," 24.

16. Alcoff, "Problem of Speaking for Others," 23

17. Spivak, *Post-Colonial Critic*, 60.

18. Alcoff, "Problem of Speaking for Others," 29.

19. Beasley-Murray, *Posthegemony*; García Canclini, *Consumers and Citizens*; Williams, *Other Side of the Popular*.

20. Derrida and Dufourmantelle, *Of Hospitality*, 59.

21. Derrida and Dufourmantelle, *Of Hospitality*, 61.

22. Crenshaw, "Mapping the Margins," 1299.

Bibliography

ABC News. "14 Illegal Immigrants Die at Ariz. Border." *ABC News*, July 18, 2001. https://abcnews.go.com/US/story?id=93225&page=1.

Acosta, Abraham. *Thresholds of Illiteracy: Theory, Latin America, and the Crisis of Resistance.* New York: Fordham University Press, 2014.

Agamben, Giorgio. *Homo Sacer: Sovereign Power and Bare Life.* Translated by Daniel Heller-Roazen. Stanford: Stanford University Press, 1998.

Agnew, Lois, et al. "Octalog III: The Politics of Historiography in 2010." *Rhetoric Review* 30, no. 2 (2011): 109–34.

Ahmed, Azam, and Kirk Semple. "Photo of Drowned Migrants Captures Pathos of Those Who Risk It All." *New York Times*, June 25, 2019. https://www.nytimes.com/2019/06/25/us/father-daughter-border-drowning-picture-mexico.html.

Alcoff, Linda. "The Problem of Speaking for Others." *Cultural Critique*, no. 20 (1991): 5–32.

Aldama, Arturo J. *Disrupting Savagism: Intersecting Chicana/o, Mexican Immigrant, and Native American Struggles for Self-Representation.* Durham: Duke University Press, 2001.

Allyn, Bobby, and Michel Marizco. "Jury Acquits Aid Worker Accused of Helping Border-Crossing Migrants in Arizona." *National Public Radio*, November 21, 2019. https://www.npr.org/2019/11/21/781658800/jury-acquits-aid-worker-accused-of-helping-border-crossing-migrants-in-arizona.

Anguiano, Claudia, and Mari Castañeda. "Forging a Path: Past and Present Scope of Critical Race Theory and Latina/o Critical Race Theory in Communication Studies." *Review of Communication* 14, no. 2 (2014): 107–24.

Anzaldúa, Gloria. *Borderlands/La Frontera: The New Mestiza.* 3rd ed. San Francisco: Aunt Lute, 1987.

Aparicio, Frances R., and Susana Chávez, eds. *Tropicalizations: Transcultural Representations of Latinidad.* Hanover: University Press of New England, 1997.

Appadurai, Arjun. *Modernity at Large: Cultural Dimensions of Globalization.* Minneapolis: University of Minnesota Press, 1996.

Archibold, Randal. C. "Arizona Enacts Stringent Law on Immigration." *New York Times*, April 23, 2010. https://www.nytimes.com/2010/04/24/us/politics/24immig.html.

Augé, Marc. *Non-places: An Introduction to Supermodernity.* New York: Verso, 1995.

Austin, Kat, and Carlos-Urani Montiel. "Codex Espangliensis: Neo-Baroque Art of Resistance." *Latin American Perspectives* 39, no. 3 (2014): 88–105.

Baca, Damián. *Mestiz@ Scripts, Digital Migrations, and the Territories of Writing.* New York: Palgrave Macmillan, 2008.

———. Preface to *Rhetorics of the Americas: 3114 BCE to 2012 CE*, edited by Damián Baca and Victor Villanueva, ix–x. New York: Palgrave Macmillan, 2010.

———. "Rethinking Composition, Five Hundred Years Later." *JAC* 29, no. 1 (2013): 229–42.

———. "Te-Ixtli: The 'Other Face' of the Americas." In *Rhetorics of the Americas: 3114 BCE to 2012 CE*, edited by Damián Baca and Victor Villanueva, 1–13. New York: Palgrave Macmillan, 2010.

Baca, Damián, and Victor Villanueva, eds. *Rhetorics of the Americas, 3114 BCE to 2012 CE.* New York: Palgrave Macmillan, 2010.

Badiou, Alain. *Ethics: An Essay on the Understanding of Evil.* New York: Verso, 2001.

Ballif, Michelle. "Regarding the Dead." *Philosophy and Rhetoric* 47, no. 4 (2014): 455–71.

Barnard, Anne, and Karam Shoumali. "Image of Drowned Syrian, Aylan Kurdi, 3, Brings Migrant Crisis into Focus." *New York Times*, September 3, 2015. https://www.nytimes.com/2015/09/04/world/europe/syria-boy-drowning.html.

Beasley-Murray, Jon. *Posthegemony: Political Theory and Latin America.* Minneapolis: University of Minnesota Press, 2010.

Béjar Lara, Adolfo. "Narrating Cross-Border Migration, Writing Subjects Without History: On Luis Alberto Urrea's *The Devil's Highway* and Francisco Cantú's *The Line Becomes a River*." *MELUS: Multi-Ethnic Literature of the U.S.* 41, no. 2 (2022): 170–91.

Bennington, Geoffrey. *Scatter 1: The Politics of Politics in Foucault, Heidegger, and Derrida.* New York: Fordham University Press, 2016.

Benson, Thomas W. "The Senses of Rhetoric: A Topical System for Critics." *Central States Speech Journal* 29, no. 4 (1978): 237–50.

Beverley, John. *Subalternity and Representation: Arguments in Cultural Theory.* Durham: Duke University Press, 1999.

Bhabha, Homi. *The Location of Culture.* New York: Routledge, 1994.

Bokser, Julie A. "Reading and Writing Sor Juana's Arch: Rhetorics of Belonging, Criollo Identity, and Feminist Histories." *Rhetoric Society Quarterly* 42, no. 2 (2012): 144–63.

———. "Sor Juana's Rhetoric of Silence." *Rhetoric Review* 25, no. 1 (2006): 5–21.

Boyce, Geoffrey Alan, Samuel N. Chambers, and Sarah Launius. "Bodily Inertia and the Weaponization of the Sonoran Desert in US Boundary Enforcement: A GIS Modeling of Migration Routes Through Arizona's Altar Valley." *Journal on Migration and Human Security* 7, no. 2 (2016): 23–35.

Brady, Mary Pat. *Extinct Lands, Temporal Geographies: Chicana Literature and the Urgency of Space.* Durham: Duke University Press, 2002.

Brewer, Jan. "Arizona Gov. Jan Brewer Explains Signing Nation's Toughest Illegal Immigration Law," *Los Angeles Times*, April 23, 2010. http://latimesblogs.latimes.com/washington/2010/04/jan-brewer-arizona-illegal-immigration.html.

Brown, Wendy. *Walled States, Waning Sovereignty.* New York: Zone Books, 2010.

Bump, Philip. "Here Are the Administration Officials Who Have Said That Family Separation Is Meant as a Deterrent." *Washington Post*, June 19, 2018. https://www.washingtonpost.com/news/politics/wp/2018/06/19/here-are-the-administration-officials-who-have-said-that-family-separation-is-meant-as-a-deterrent/.

Burke, Kenneth. *Attitudes Toward History.* 3rd ed. Berkeley: University of California Press, 1984.

———. *Language as Symbolic Action: Essays on Life, Literature, and Method.* Berkeley: University of California Press, 1966.

———. *A Rhetoric of Motives.* Berkeley: University of California Press, 1969.

Butler, Judith, and Gayatri Chakravorty Spivak. *Who Sings the Nation-State? Language, Politics, Belonging.* New York: Seagull, 2011.

Cacho, Lisa Marie. *Social Death: Racialized Rightlessness and the Criminalization of the Unprotected.* New York: New York University Press, 2012.

Calafell, Bernadette Marie. "Disrupting the Dichotomy: 'Yo Soy Chicana/o?' In the New Latina/o South." *Communication Review* 7, no. 2 (2004): 175–204.

Calderón, Héctor, and José David Saldívar, eds. *Criticism in the Borderlands: Studies in Chicano Literature, Culture, and Ideology.* Durham: Duke University Press, 1991.

Camacho, Alicia Schmidt. *Migrant Imaginaries: Latino Cultural Politics in the U.S.-Mexico Borderlands*. New York: New York University Press, 2008.

Cantú, Francisco. *The Line Becomes a River: Dispatches from the Border*. New York: Riverhead Books, 2018.

Cárdenas, Maritza E. *Constituting Central American-Americans: Transnational Identities and the Politics of Dislocation*. New Brunswick: Rutgers University Press, 2018.

Carrera, Magali M. *Imagining Identity in New Spain: Race, Lineage, and the Colonial Body in Portraiture and Casta Paintings*. Austin: University of Texas Press, 2003.

Castillo, Debra A., and María Socorro Tabuenca Córdoba. *Border Women: Writing from La Frontera*. Minneapolis: University of Minnesota Press, 2002.

Chandler, Nahum Dimitri. *X: The Problem of the Negro as a Problem for Thought*. New York: Fordham University Press, 2014.

Chávez, Karma R. "Border (In)Securities: Normative and Differential Belonging in LGBTQ and Immigrant Rights Discourse." *Communication and Critical/Cultural Studies* 7, no. 2 (2010): 136–55.

———. "Embodied Translation: Dominant Discourse and Communication with Migrant Bodies-as-Text." *Howard Journal of Communications* 20 (2009): 18–36.

———. *Queer Migrations: Activist Rhetoric and Coalitional Possibilities*. Urbana: University of Illinois Press, 2013.

Chávez, Karma R., and Hana Masri. "The Rhetoric of Family in the U.S. Immigration Movement: A Queer Migration Analysis of the 2014 Central American Child Migrant 'Crisis.'" In *Queer and Trans Migrations: Dynamics of Illegalization, Detention, and Deportation*, edited by Eithne Luibhéid and Karma R. Chávez, 208–225. Urbana: University of Illinois Press, 2020.

Chavez, Leo R. *The Latino Threat: Constructing Immigrants, Citizens, and the Nation*. Stanford: Stanford University Press, 2008.

Chirindo, Kundai. "Rhetorical Places: From Classical Topologies to Prospects for Post-Westphalian Spatialities," *Women's Studies in Communication* 39, no. 2 (2016): 127–31.

Christensen, Francis. *Notes Toward a New Rhetoric*. New York: Harper and Row, 1967.

Cintrón, Ralph. "Democracy and Its Limitations." In *The Public Work of Rhetoric: Citizen-Scholars and Civic Engagement*, edited by John M. Ackerman and David J. Coogan, 98–116. Columbia: University of South Carolina Press, 2010.

Cisneros, Josue David. *The Border Crossed Us: Rhetorics of Borders, Citizenship, and Latina/o Identity*. Tuscaloosa: University of Alabama Press, 2014.

Clinton, William J. "Remarks and an Exchange with Reporters on Immigration Policy." In *Public Papers of the Presidents of the United States: William J. Clinton, 1993, Book I*, 1194–195. Washington, DC: U.S. Government Printing Office, 1994. https://www.govinfo.gov/content/pkg/PPP-1993-book1/pdf/PPP-1993-book1-doc-pg1194.pdf.

Cole, Teju. "A Crime Scene at the Border." *New York Times*, July 10, 2019. https://www.nytimes.com/2019/07/10/magazine/drowned-migrants-photo-us-mexico-border.html.

Consigny, Scott. "Rhetoric and Its Situations." *Philosophy and Rhetoric* 7, no. 3 (1974): 175–86.

Cope, Douglas R. *The Limits of Racial Domination: Plebeian Society in Colonial Mexico City, 1660–1720*. Madison: University of Wisconsin Press, 1994.

Corder, Jim W. "Argument as Emergence, Rhetoric as Love." *Rhetoric Review* 4, no. 1 (1985): 16–32.

Cornelius, Wayne A. "Death at the Border: Efficacy and Unintended Consequences of US Immigration Control Policy." *Population and Development Review* 27, no. 4 (2001): 661–85.

Corradini, Michael, Jonathan Allen Kringen, Laura Simich, Karen Berberich, and Meredith Emigh. *Operation Streamline: No Evidence That Criminal Prosecution Deters Migration*. New York: Vera Institute of Justice, 2018. https://www.vera.org/downloads /publications/operation_streamline-report.pdf.

Cortez, José M., and Romeo García. "The Absolute Limit of Latinx Writing." *College Composition and Communication* 70, no. 4 (2020): 566–90.

Crenshaw, Kimberlé. "Mapping the Margins: Intersectionality, Identity Politics, and Violence Against Women of Color." *Stanford Law Review* 43, no. 6 (1991): 1241–99.

Davis, Diane. *Inessential Solidarity: Rhetoric and Foreigner Relations*. Pittsburgh: University of Pittsburgh Press, 2010.

DeChaine, D. Robert, ed. *Border Rhetorics: Citizenship and Identity on the US-Mexico Frontier*. Tuscaloosa: University of Alabama Press, 2012.

———. "Introduction: For Rhetorical Border Studies." In *Border Rhetorics: Citizenship and Identity on the US-Mexico Frontier*, edited by D. Robert DeChaine, 1–15. Tuscaloosa: University of Alabama Press, 2012.

De Genova, Nicholas. "Anonymous Brown Bodies: The Productive Power of the Deadly U.S.-Mexico Border." In *Migration and Mortality: Social Death, Dispossession, and Survival in the Americas*, edited by Jamie Longazel and Miranda Cady Hallett, 83–100. Philadelphia: Temple University Press, 2021.

DeLanda, Manuel. *A New Philosophy of Society: Assemblage Theory and Social Complexity*. London: Continuum, 2006.

De León, Jason. *The Land of Open Graves: Living and Dying on the Migrant Trail*. Oakland: University of California Press, 2015.

Deleuze, Gilles. *Difference and Repetition*. Translated by Paul Patton. New York: Columbia University Press, 1994.

———. "Postscript on the Societies of Control." *October* 59 (1992): 3–7.

Derrida, Jacques. *Of Grammatology*. Translated by Gayatri Chakravorty Spivak. Baltimore: Johns Hopkins University Press, 1976.

———. *Rogues: Two Essays on Reason*. Translated by Pascale-Anne Brault and Michael Naas. Stanford: Stanford University Press, 2005.

———. *The Truth in Painting*. Translated by Geoff Bennington and Ian McLeod. Chicago: University of Chicago Press, 1987.

Derrida, Jacques, and Anne Dufourmantelle. *Of Hospitality*. Translated by Rachel Bowlby. Stanford: Stanford University Press, 2000.

Diaz, Tony. "I Am a Book Trafficker." *CNN*, March 12, 2012. https://www.cnn.com/2012 /03/12/us/opinion-i-am-a-book-trafficker/index.html.

Dickerson, Caitlin. "Parents of 545 Children Separated at the Border Cannot Be Found." *New York Times*, October 21, 2020. https://www.nytimes.com/2020/10/21/us/migrant -children-separated.html#::text=It%20is%20now%20clear%20that,were%20separated %2C%20the%20documents%20show.

Doty, Roxanne L. "Bare Life: Border-Crossing Deaths and Spaces of Moral Alibi." *Environment and Planning D: Society and Space* 29, no. 4 (2011): 599–612.

Dunn, Timothy J. *Blockading the Border and Human Rights: The El Paso Operation That Remade Immigration Enforcement*. Austin: University of Texas Press, 2009.

Dussel, Enrique. "Eurocentrism and Modernity (Introduction to the Frankfurt Lectures)." In *The Postmodernism Debate in Latin America*, edited by John Beverley, Michael Aronna, and José Oviedo, 65–76. Durham: Duke University Press, 1995.

Eide, Tormond. "Aristotelian Topos and Greek Geometry," *Symbolae Osloenses* 70, no. 1 (1995): 5–21.

Ekstrand, Laurie E. *Border Control: Revised Strategy Is Showing Some Positive Results.* GAO/ GGD-95-30. Washington, DC: Government Accountability Office, 1994. https:// www.gao.gov/assets/ggd-95-30.pdf.

Enoch, Jessica. "Survival Stories: Feminist Historiographic Approaches to Chicana Rhetorics of Sterilization Abuse." *Rhetoric Society Quarterly* 35, no. 3 (2009): 5–30.

Esteva-Fabregat, Claudio. *Mestizaje in Ibero-America.* Translated by John Wheat. Tucson: University of Arizona Press, 1995.

Ettinger, Patrick. "'We Sometimes Wonder What They Will Spring on Us Next': Immigrants and Border Enforcement in the American West, 1882–1930." *Western Historical Quarterly* 37, no. 2 (2006): 159–81.

Fan, Mary D. "When Deterrence and Death Mitigation Fall Short: Fantast and Fetishes as Gap-Fillers in Border Regulation." *Law and Society Review* 42, no. 4 (2008): 708–34.

Farrell, Thomas B. "The Weight of Rhetoric: Studies in Cultural Delirium." *Philosophy and Rhetoric* 41, no. 4 (2008): 467–87.

Fernandez, Manny. "A Path to America, Marked by More and More Bodies." *New York Times.* May 4, 2017. https://www.nytimes.com/interactive/2017/05/04/us/texas-border -migrants-dead-bodies.html.

Fieser, Ezra. "What Do 'Social Inclusion' Rankings Tell Us About the Child Migrant Crisis?" *Christian Science Monitor.* July 29, 2014. https://www.csmonitor.com/World/Americas /2014/0729/What-do-social-inclusion-rankings-tell-us-about-the-child-migrant -crisis/Dramatic-social-disparity-across-the-Americas.

Fisher, T. G. "Don't Force Me to Mourn (or Pay) for Dead Illegal Immigrants." *Arizona Republic,* December 20, 2017. https://www.azcentral.com/story/news/politics/border-issues /2017/12/14/investigation-border-patrol-undercounts-deaths-border-crossing -migrants/933689001/.

Fleischer, Ari. "On Fox, Ari Fleischer Says Dead Migrant Father and Daughter Should Have Come Here Legally. They Tried, but Were Turned Away." *Media Matters for America,* June 26, 2019. https://www.mediamatters.org/fox-news/fox-ari-fleischer-says-dead -migrant-father-and-daughter-should-have-come-here-legally-they.

Flores, Lisa A. "Constructing Rhetorical Borders: Peons, Illegal Aliens, and Competing Narratives of Immigration." *Critical Studies in Media Communication* 20, no. 4 (2003): 362–87.

———. *Deportable and Disposable: Public Rhetoric and the Making of the "Illegal" Immigrant.* University Park: Pennsylvania State University Press, 2020.

———. "Stoppage and the Racialized Rhetorics of Mobility." *Western Journal of Communication* 84, no. 3 (2020): 247–63.

Flores, Nelson, and Jonathan Rosa. "Undoing Appropriateness: Raciolinguistic Ideologies and Language Diversity in Education." *Harvard Educational Review* 85, no. 2 (2015): 149–72.

Flores, William V., and Rina Benmayor, eds. *Latino Cultural Citizenship: Claiming Identity, Space, and Rights.* Boston: Beacon, 1998.

Foucault, Michel. *The History of Sexuality, Volume 1: An Introduction.* Translated by Robert Hurley. New York: Pantheon Books, 1978.

———. *Lectures on the Will to Know: Lectures at the Collège de France, 1970–1971, and Oedipal Knowledge.* Edited by Daniel Defert. Translated by Graham Burchell. New York: Palgrave Macmillan, 2013.

———. *The Order of Things: An Archaeology of the Human Sciences.* New York: Vintage Books, 1994.

Fredrick, James. "'Metering' at the Border." *National Public Radio,* June 29, 2019. https://www .npr.org/2019/06/29/737268856/metering-at-the-border.

García, María Cristina. *Seeking Refuge: Central American Migration to Mexico, the United States, and Canada*. Berkeley: University of California Press, 2006.

García, M. T. *Desert Immigrants: The Mexicans of El Paso, 1880–1920*. New Haven: Yale University Press, 1982.

García, Romeo, and José M. Cortez. "The Trace of a Mark That Scatters: The Anthropoi and the Rhetoric of Decoloniality." *Rhetoric Society Quarterly* 50, no. 2 (2020): 93–108.

García Canclini, Néstor. *Consumers and Citizens: Globalization and Multicultural Conflicts*. Translated by George Yúdice. Minneapolis: University of Minnesota Press, 2001.

Gómez-Peña, Guillermo. *Dangerous Border Crossers: The Artist Talks Back*. New York: Routledge, 2000.

Gómez-Peña, Guillermo, Enrique Chagoya, and Felicia Rice. *Codex Espangliensis: From Columbus to the Border Patrol*. San Francisco: City Lights Books, 2000.

Goodwin, Gretta L. *Immigration Enforcement: Immigration-Related Prosecutions Increased from 2017 to 2018 in Response to U.S. Attorney General's Direction*. GAO-20-172. Washington, DC: Government Accountability Office, 2019. https://www.gao.gov/assets/710/706519.pdf.

Graff Zivin, Erin. *Anarchaeologies: Reading as Misreading*. New York: Fordham University Press, 2020.

Gramsci, Antonio. *Selections from the Prison Notebooks of Antonio Gramsci*. Edited and translated by Quintin Hoare and Geoffrey Nowell Smith. New York: International, 1971.

Grosfoguel, Ramón. "Decolonizing Post-Colonial Studies and Paradigms of Political Economy: Transmodernity, Decolonial Thinking, and Global Coloniality." *Transmodernity* 1, no. 1 (2011): 1–37.

Guardian. "Kamala Harris Tells Migrants 'Do Not Come' During Talks in Guatemala." YouTube, June 07, 2021. https://www.youtube.com/watch?v=bpGitFIzamQ.

Guha, Ranajit. "The Prose of Counter-Insurgency." In *Selected Subaltern Studies*, edited by Ranajit Guha and Gayatri Chakravorty Spivak, 45–86. New York: Oxford University Press, 1988.

Guidotti-Hernández, Nicole. *Unspeakable Violence: Remapping U.S. and Mexican National Imaginaries*. Durham: Duke University Press, 2011.

Gutiérrez, David, G. *Walls and Mirrors: Mexican Americans, Mexican Immigrants, and the Politics of Ethnicity*. Berkeley: University of California Press, 1995.

Guzmán, R. Andrés. *Universal Citizenship: Latina/o Studies at the Limits of Identity*. Austin: University of Texas Press, 2019.

Hardt, Michael. "The Withering of Civil Society." *Social Text* 45 (1995): 27–44.

Hartelius, E. Johanna, ed. *The Rhetorics of US Immigration: Identity, Community, Otherness*. University Park: Pennsylvania State University Press, 2015.

Hatfield, Charles. *The Limits of Identity: Politics and Poetics in Latin America*. Austin: University of Texas Press, 2015.

Hernández, Kelly Lytle. *Bad Mexicans: Race, Empire, and Revolution in the Borderlands*. New York: Norton, 2022.

———. *Migra! A History of the U.S. Border Patrol*. Berkeley: University of California Press, 2010.

Hernández Cuevas, Marco Polo. "The Mexican Colonial Term 'Chino' Is a Referent of Afrodescendant." *Journal of Pan African Studies* 5, no. 5 (2012): 124–43.

Hing, Bill Ong. *American Presidents, Deportations, and Human Rights Violations: From Carter to Trump*. Cambridge: Cambridge University Press, 2018.

Horne, Tom. "An Open Letter to the Citizens of Tucson." June 11, 2007. www.scribd.com/doc/32001977/AnOpen-Letter-to-the-citizens-of-Tucson.

Howes, Franny. "Imagining a Multiplicity of Visual Rhetorical Traditions: Comics Lessons from Rhetoric Histories." *ImageText* 5, no. 3 (2010–11). https:// imagetextjournal.com /imagining-a-multiplicity-of-visual-rhetorical-traditions-comics-lessons-from -rhetoric-histories/.

Huffington Post. "U.S. Deports Honduran Children in First Flight Since Obama's Pledge." July 14, 2014. https://www.huffpost.com/entry/us-deports-honduran-children_n _5586326.

Hulse, Carl. "Immigrant Surge Rooted in Law to Curb Child Trafficking." *New York Times,* July 7, 2014. https://www.nytimes.com/2014/07/08/us/immigrant-surge-rooted-in -law-to-curb-child-trafficking.html.

Hunter, Tera W. "The Long History of Child Snatching." *New York Times,* June 3, 2018. https://www.nytimes.com/2018/06/03/opinion/children-border.html.

International Organization for Migration. "US-Mexico Border the World's Deadliest Migration Land Route." September 12, 2023. https://www.iom.int/news/us-mexico-border -worlds-deadliest-migration-land-route#::text=Geneva%2FBerlin%2FSan %20Jos%C3%A9%20%E2%80%93,for%20migrants%20worldwide%20on%20record.

Izaguirre, José G., III. "'A Social Movement in Fact': *La Raza* and *El Plan de Delano*." *Rhetoric Society Quarterly* 50, no. 1 (2020): 53–68.

Johnson, Carrie. "Probe Finds Arizona Sheriff Violated Civil Rights." *National Public Radio,* December 15, 2011. https://www.npr.org/2019/11/21/781658800/jury-acquits-aid -worker-accused-of-helping-border-crossing-migrants-in-arizona.

Jordan, Miriam. "Family Members Separated at Border May Each Get Up to $450,000." *New York Times,* October 28, 2021. https://www.nytimes.com/2021/10/28/us/politics /trump-family-separation-border.html.

———. "'I Have No Idea Where My Daughter Is': Migrant Parents Are Desperate for News." *New York Times,* April 9, 2021. https://www.nytimes.com/2021/04/09/us/migrant -children-border-parents.html.

Katzew, Ilona. *Casta Painting: Images of Race in Eighteenth-Century Mexico.* New Haven: Yale University Press, 2004.

Kelly, Caroline, Catherine E. Shoichet, and Priscilla Alvarez. "Ken Cuccinelli Blames Drowned Man in Border Photograph for Own, Daughters, Deaths." *CNN,* June 27, 2019. https://www.cnn.com/2019/06/27/politics/ken-cuccinelli-drowned-father-daughter -fault/index.html.

Kennerly, Michele. "Atopos." In *A New Handbook of Rhetoric: Inverting the Classical Vocabulary,* edited by Michele Kennerly, 53–71. University Park: Pennsylvania State University Press, 2021.

Latin American Subaltern Studies Group. "Founding Statement." *Boundary* 20, no. 3 (1993): 110–21.

Lechuga, Maria, and Antonio Tomas De La Garza. "Forum: Border Rhetorics." *Communication and Critical/Cultural Studies* 18, no. 1 (2021): 37–40.

Le Duc, Julia. "Migrante Salvadoreño y su hija mueren en el intento de cruzar a EU." *La Jornada.* June 25, 2019. https://www.jornada.com.mx/sin-fronteras/2019/06/24 /migrante-salvadoreno-y-su-hija-mueren-en-el-intento-de-cruzar-a-eu-9107.html.

Leff, Michael. "Up from Theory: Or I Fought the Topoi and the Topoi Won." *Rhetoric Society Quarterly* 36, no. 2 (2006): 203–11.

Legal Information Institute. "6 U.S. Code § 279—Children's Affairs." Cornell Law School. Accessed November 9, 2021. https://www.law.cornell.edu/uscode/text/6/279#g_2.

———. "8 U.S. Code § 1325—Improper entry by alien." Cornell Law School. Accessed November 9, 2021. https://www.law.cornell.edu/uscode/text/6/279#g_2.

Lim, Julian. *Porous Borders: Multiracial Migrations and the Law in the US–Mexico Border-lands*. Chapel Hill: University of North Carolina Press, 2017.

Lugones, María. *Pilgrimages/Peregrinajes: Theorizing Coalition Against Multiple Oppressions*. Lanham, MD: Rowman and Littlefield, 2003.

———. "Toward a Decolonial Feminism." *Hypatia* 25, no. 4 (2010): 742–59.

Luiselli, Valeria. *Tell Me How It Ends: An Essay in Forty Questions*. Minneapolis: Coffee House, 2017.

Lund, Joshua. "Barbarian Theorizing and the Limits of Latin American Exceptionalism." *Cultural Critique* 47, no. 1 (2001): 54–90.

Lunsford, Andrea. "Toward a Mestiza Rhetoric: Gloria Anzaldúa on Composition and Post-coloniality." *JAC* 18, no. 1 (1998): 1–27.

Lyotard, Jean-François. *The Differend: Phrases in Dispute*. Translated by Georges Van Den Abbeele. Minneapolis: University of Minnesota Press, 1988.

Makoni, Sinfree, and Alastair Pennycook. "Disinventing and (Re)Constituting Languages." *Critical Inquiry in Language Studies* 2, no. 3 (2005): 137–56.

Maldonado, José Ángel. "Manifestx: Toward a Rhetoric Loaded with Future." *Communication and Critical/Cultural Studies* 17, no. 1 (2020): 104–10.

———. "Rhetorical Rumors: Hauntology in International Feminicidio Discourse." In *Networking Argument*, edited by Carol Winkler, 388–93. New York: Routledge, 2020.

Mallon, Florencia. "The Promise and Dilemma of Subaltern Studies: Perspectives from Latin American History." *American Historical Review* 99 (1994): 1491–1515.

Mao, LuMing. "Doing Comparative Rhetoric Responsibly." *Rhetoric Society Quarterly* 41, no. 1 (2011): 64–69.

Mao, LuMing, Bo Wang, Arabella Lyon, Susan C. Jarratt, C. Jan Swearingen, Susan Romano, Peter Simonson, Steven Mailloux, and Xing Lu. "Manifesting a Future for Comparative Rhetoric." *Rhetoric Review* 34, no. 3 (2015): 239–74.

Márquez, John D. "Latinos as the 'Living Dead': Raciality, Expendability, and Border Militarization." *Latino Studies* 10 (2012): 473–98.

Martin, Jerry. "How 1994's Operation Gatekeeper Made Border Patrol Better and Ended the 'Chaos.'" *San Diego Union-Tribune*, September 30, 2019. https://www.sandiegounion tribune.com/2019/09/30/how-1994s-operation-gatekeeper-made-border-patrol -better-and-ended-the-chaos/.

Martínez, Daniel E., Robin C. Reineke, Geoffrey Boyce, Samuel N. Chambers, Sarah Launius, Bruce E. Anderson, Gregory L. Hess, Jennifer M. Vollner, Bruce O. Parks, Caitlin C. M. Vogelsberg, Gabriella Soto, Michael Kreyche, and Raquel Rubio-Goldsmith. *Migrant Deaths in Southern Arizona: Recovered Undocumented Border Crosser Remains Investigated by the Pima County Office of the Medical Examiner, 1990–2020*. Binational Migration Institute, University of Arizona, 2021. https://sbs.arizona.edu/sites/sbs.arizona.edu /files/BMI%20Report%202021%20ENGLISH_FINAL.pdf.

Martínez, Daniel E., Robin C. Reineke, Raquel Rubio-Goldsmith, and Bruce O. Parks. "Structural Violence and Migrant Deaths in Southern Arizona: Data from the Pima County Office of the Medical Examiner, 1990–2013." *Journal on Migration and Human Security* 2, no. 4 (2014): 257–86.

Martínez, Maria Elena. *Genealogical Fictions: Limpieza de Sangre, Religion, and Gender in Colonial Mexico*. Stanford: Stanford University Press, 2008.

Massey, Douglas S. "Borderline Madness: America's Counterproductive Immigration Policy." In *Debating Immigration*, edited by Carol M. Swain, 129–37. Cambridge: Cambridge University Press, 2007.

Massey Douglas S., and Karen A. Pren. "Unintended Consequences of US Immigration Policy: Explaining the Post-1965 Surge from Latin America." *Population and Development Review* 38 (2012): 1–29.

Massey, Douglas S., Karen A. Pren, and Jorge Durand. "Why Border Enforcement Backfired." *American Journal of Sociology* 121, no. 5 (2016): 1557–1600.

Masuoka, Natalie, and Jane Junn. *The Politics of Belonging: Race, Public Opinion, and Immigration.* Chicago: University of Chicago Press, 2013.

McKeon, Richard. "Creativity and the Commonplace." *Philosophy and Rhetoric* 6, no. 4 (1973): 199–210.

Medina, Cruz. *Reclaiming Poch@ Pop: Examining the Rhetoric of Cultural Deficiency.* New York: Palgrave Macmillan, 2015.

Meissner, Doris, and Donald Kerwin. 2009. *DHS and Immigration: Taking Stock and Correcting Course.* Washington, DC: Migration Policy Institute. https://immigrationresearch .org/system/files/MPI_DHS_and_Immigration-Taking_Stock_and_Correcting _Course.pdf.

Mendieta, Eduardo, and Guillermo Gómez-Peña. "A Latino Philosopher Interviews a Chicano Performance Artist." *Neplanta: Views from South* 2, no. 3 (2001): 539–54.

Mignolo, Walter D. "Colonial and Postcolonial Discourse: Cultural Critique or Academic Colonialism?" *Latin American Research Review* 28, no. 3 (1993): 120–34.

———. *The Darker Side of the Renaissance: Literacy, Territoriality, and Colonization.* Ann Arbor: University of Michigan Press, 1995.

———. "Delinking: The Rhetoric of Modernity, the Logic of Coloniality, and the Grammar of De-Coloniality." *Cultural Studies* 21, no. 2 (2007): 449–514.

———. "The Geopolitics of Knowledge and the Colonial Difference." *South Atlantic Quarterly* 101, no. 1 (2002): 57–96.

———. *Local Histories/Global Designs: Coloniality, Subaltern Knowledges, and Border Thinking.* Durham: Duke University Press, 2000.

Mignolo, Walter, and Madina V. Tlostanova. "Theorizing from the Borders: Shifting to Geo- and Body-Politics of Knowledge." *European Journal of Social Theory* 9, no. 2 (2006): 205–21.

Miller, Carolyn R. "Aristotle's 'Special Topics' in Rhetorical Practice and Pedagogy." *Rhetoric Society Quarterly* 17, no. 1 (1987): 61–70.

Miller, Todd. *Border Patrol Nation: Dispatches from the Front Lines of Homeland Security.* San Francisco: City Lights Books, 2014.

Miroff, Nick, and Sari Horwitz. "Trump Didn't Invent Family Separation, but His Administration Was Willing to Try It." *Washington Post*, June 19, 2018. https://www.washington post.com/world/national-security/trump-didnt-invent-family-separation-but-his -administration-was-eager-to-try-it/2018/06/19/f32f11f6–73d6–11e8-b4b7–3084002 42c2e_story.html.

Modern Language Association. "Statement on Tucson Mexican American Studies Program." Public statement by Executive Council, February 2012. https://www.mla.org/Resources /Advocacy/Executive-Council-Actions/2012/Statement-on-Tucson-Mexican -American-Studies-Program.

Molina, Natalia. *How Race Is Made in America: Immigration, Citizenship, and the Historical Power of Racial Scripts.* Berkeley: University of California Press, 2014.

Moreiras, Alberto. *The Exhaustion of Difference: The Politics of Latin American Cultural Studies.* Durham: Duke University Press, 2001.

Mukasey, Michael, and Michael Chertoff. "Transcript of State of the Border Press Conference with Attorney General Michael Mukasey and Homeland Security Secretary

Michael Chertoff." U.S. Department of Justice, February 22, 2008. https://www
.justice.gov/archive/opa/pr/2008/February/08_opa_138.html.

Muñoz, José Esteban. *Disidentifications: Queers of Color and the Performance of Politics*. Minneapolis: University of Minnesota Press, 1999.

Murphy, James J., James Berlin, Robert J. Connors, Sharon Crowley, Richard Leo Enos, Victor
J. Vitanza, Susan C. Jarratt, Nan Johnson, and Jan Swearingen. "The Politics of Historiography." *Rhetoric Review* 7, no. 1 (1988): 5–49.

Nancy, Jean-Luc. *The Inoperative Community*. Translated by Peter Connor, Lisa Garbus,
Michael Holland, and Simona Sawhney. Minneapolis: University of Minnesota
Press, 1991.

Negri, Antonio. "Twenty Theses on Marx, Interpretation of the Class Situation Today." In
Marxism Beyond Marxism, edited by Saree Makdisi, Cesare Casarino, and Rebecca E.
Karl, 149–80. New York: Routledge, 1996.

Nevins, Joseph. *Operation Gatekeeper: The Rise of the Illegal Alien and the Remaking of the
U.S.-Mexico Boundary*. New York: Routledge, 2002.

Ngai, Mae M. "The Strange Career of the Illegal Alien: Immigration Restrictions and Deportation Policy in the United States, 1921–1965." *Law and History Review* 21, no. 1 (2003):
69–107.

No More Deaths and La Coalición de Derechos Humanos. *The Disappeared Report Part 3:
Left to Die: Border Patrol, Search and Rescue, and the Crisis of Disappearance*. February 3,
2021. http://www.thedisappearedreport.org/uploads/8/3/5/1/83515082/left_to_die_
-_english.pdf.

Ochoa O'Leary, Anna, Andrea J. Romero, Nolan L. Cabrera, and Michelle Rascón. "Assault
on Ethnic Studies." In *Arizona Firestorm: Global Immigration Realities, National Media,
and Provincial Politics*, ed. Otto Santa Ana, and Celeste González de Bustamante,
97–122. Lanham, MD: Rowman and Littlefield, 2012.

O'Dell, Rob, Daniel González, and Jill Castellano. "'Mass Disaster' Grows at the U.S.-
Mexico Border, but Washington Doesn't Seem to Care." *Arizona Republic*, December
20, 2017. https://www.azcentral.com/story/news/politics/border-issues/2017/12/14
/investigation-border-patrol-undercounts-deaths-border-crossing-migrants
/933689001/.

Olson, Christa J. *Constitutive Visions: Indigeneity and Commonplaces of National Identity in
Republican Ecuador*. University Park: Penn State University Press, 2014.

———. "Cruel Looking: From Puerto Rico, and Beyond." *Reading the Pictures*, December 17,
2017. https://www.readingthepictures.org/2017/12/cruel-looking/.

———. "Places to Stand: The Practices and Politics of Writing Histories." *Advances in the
History of Rhetoric* 15 (2012): 77–100.

Olson, Christa J., and René Agustín de los Santos. "Expanding the Idea of América." *Rhetoric
Society Quarterly* 45, no. 3 (2015): 193–98.

Ono, Kent A., and John M. Sloop. *Shifting Borders: Rhetoric, Immigration, and California's
Proposition 187*. Philadelphia: Temple University Press, 2002.

Ore, Ersula. *Lynching: Violence, Rhetoric, and American Identity*. Jackson: University of Mis-
sissippi Press, 2019.

———. "They Call Me Dr. Ore." *Present Tense* 5, no. 2 (2015). http://www.presenttensejournal
.org/volume-5/they-call-me-dr-ore/.

Oxford English Dictionary. s.v. "deter (v.)." Accessed October 22, 2020. https://www.oed.com
/dictionary/deter_v1?tab=meaning_and_use#7051083.

Parra, Carlos Francisco. "Valientes Nogalenses: The 1918 Battle Between the U.S. and Mexico that Transformed Ambos Nogales." *Journal of Arizona History* 51, no. 1 (2010):
1–32.

Pérez, Emma. *The Decolonial Imaginary: Writing Chicanas into History*. Bloomington: Indiana University Press, 1999.

Perry, Rick. "What Obama Missed on the Border." *Wall Street Journal*, July 15, 2014. https://www.wsj.com/articles/rick-perry-what-obama-missed-on-the-border-1405469050.

Planas, Roque. "Trump's Family Separation Policy Aims to Deter Immigration. That May Make It Illegal." *Huffington Post*, June 7, 2018. https://www.huffpost.com/entry/trumps-family-separation-policy-is-meant-to-deter-immigration-that-could-make-it-illegal_n_5b194b89e4b0599bc6e17605.

Poblete, Juan, ed. *Critical Latin American and Latino Studies*. Minneapolis: University of Minnesota Press, 2003.

Ramírez, Cristina. *Occupying Our Space: The Mestiza Rhetorics of Mexican Women Journalists and Activists, 1875–1942*. Tucson: University of Arizona Press, 2015.

Rancière, Jacques. *Disagreement: Politics and Philosophy*. Translated by Julie Rose. Minneapolis: University of Minnesota Press, 1999.

Ratcliffe, Krista. *Rhetorical Listening: Identification, Gender, Whiteness*. Carbondale: Southern Illinois University Press, 2005.

Reeves, Joshua. "Suspended Identification: *Atopos* and the Work of Public Memory." *Philosophy and Rhetoric* 46, no. 3 (2013): 306–27.

Ribero, Ana Milena. *Dreamer Nation: Immigration, Activism, and Neoliberalism*. Tuscaloosa: University of Alabama Press, 2023.

Rice, Felicia, Guillermo Gómez-Peña, Jennifer A. González, Gustavo Vazquez, and Zachary James Watkins. *Documentado/Undocumented: Ars Shamánica Performática*. San Francisco: City Lights Books, 2017.

Roberts, Laurie. "Here's How GOP Can Get Back at Obama on Immigration." *Arizona Republic*, November 17, 2014. https://www.azcentral.com/story/laurieroberts/2014/11/17/obama-unveils-immigration-plan-this-week/19044863/.

Rodríguez, Ileana. "Reading Subalterns Across Texts, Disciplines, and Theories: From Representation to Recognition." In *The Latin American Subaltern Studies Reader*, edited by Ileana Rodriguez, 1–34. Durham: Duke University Press, 2001.

Rodríguez Matos, Jaime. "After the Ruin of Thinking: From Locationalism to Infrapolitics." *Transmodernity* 5, no. 1 (2015): 1–8.

Romney, Abraham. "Indian Ability (Auilidad de Indio) and Rhetoric's Civilizing Narrative: Guaman Poma's Contact with the Rhetorical Tradition." *College Composition and Communication* 63, no. 1 (2011): 12–34.

———. "Rhetoric from the Margins: Juan Francisco Manzano's *Autobiografía de un Esclavo*." *Rhetoric Society Quarterly* 45, no. 3 (2015): 237–49.

Rosaldo, Renato. *Culture and Truth: The Remaking of Social Analysis*. Boston: Beacon, 1989.

Rosas, Gilberto. "The Managed Violences of the Borderlands: Treacherous Geographies, Policeability, and the Politics of Race." *Latino Studies* 4, no. 4 (2006): 401–18.

Saldaña-Portillo, María Josefina. *Indian Given: Racial Geographies Across Mexico and the United States*. Durham: Duke University Press, 2016.

———. "The Violence of Citizenship in the Making of Refugees." *Social Text* 37, no. 4 (2019): 1–24.

Saldívar, José David. *Border Matters: Remapping American Cultural Studies*. Berkeley: University of California Press, 1997.

Sandia National Laboratories. *Systematic Analysis of the Southwest Border Volume 1*. Washington, DC: U.S. Department of Homeland Security, 1993. https://www.dhs.gov/sites/default/files/publications/systematic-analysis-of-southwest-border-vol-1.pdf.

Sandoval, Chela. *Methodology of the Oppressed*. Minneapolis: University of Minnesota Press, 2000.

Scott, James. *Domination and the Arts of Resistance: Hidden Transcripts*. New Haven: Yale University Press, 1990.

Shakira. "The Parents of 545 Children Are Missing, and the Silence Is Blaring." *Time*, October 30, 2020. https://time.com/5905371/shakira-child-separation-border/.

Shome, Raka. "Postcolonial Interventions in the Rhetorical Canon: An 'Other' View." In *Contemporary Rhetorical Theory: A Reader*, edited by John Louis Lucaites, Celeste Michelle Condit, and Sally Caudill, 591–608. New York: Guilford, 1999.

Sowards, Stacey K. "Rhetoricity of Borders: Whiteness in Latinidad and Beyond." *Communication and Critical/Cultural Studies* 18, no. 1 (2021): 41–49.

Spivak, Gayatri Chakravorty. "Can the Subaltern Speak?" In *Marxism and the Interpretation of Culture*, edited by Cary Nelson and Lawrence Grossberg, 271–313. Urbana: University of Illinois Press, 1988.

———. "Deconstructing Historiography." In *Selected Subaltern Studies*, edited by Ranajit Guha and Gayatri Chakravorty Spivak, 3–32. New York: Oxford University Press, 1988.

———. *The Post-Colonial Critic: Interviews, Strategies, Dialogues*. Edited by Sarah Harasym. New York: Routledge, 1990.

Spivak, Gayatri Chakravorty, Philip Sipiora, and Janet Atwill. "Rhetoric and Cultural Explanation: A Discussion with Gayatri Chakravorty Spivak." *JAC* 10, no. 2 (1990): 293–313.

Stana, Richard M. *Illegal Immigration: Status of Southwest Border Strategy Implementation*. GAO/GGD-99-44. Washington, DC: Government Accountability Office, 1999. www.gao.gov/assets/ggd-99-44.pdf.

Stavans, Ilan. *The Hispanic Condition: Reflections on Culture and Identity in America*. New York: HarperCollins, 1995.

Stephen, Lynn. "*Los nuevos desaparecidos*: Immigration, Militarization, Death, and Disappearance on Mexico's Borders." In *Security Disarmed: Critical Perspectives on Gender, Race, and Militarization*, edited by Barbara Sutton, Sandra Morgen, and Julie Novkov, 122–58. New Brunswick: Rutgers University Press, 2008.

Sterngold, James. "Devastating Picture of Immigrants, Dead in Arizona Desert." *New York Times*, May 25, 2001. https://www.nytimes.com/2001/05/25/us/devastating-picture-of-immigrants-dead-in-arizona-desert.html.

St. John, Rachel. *Line in the Sand: A History of the Western U.S.-Mexico Border*. Princeton: Princeton University Press, 2011.

———. "The Raging Controversy at the Border Began with This Incident 100 Years Ago." *Smithsonian Magazine*, July 2018. https://www.smithsonianmag.com/history/raging-controversy-border-began-100-years-ago-180969343/.

Stroud, Scott R. "Pragmatism and the Methodology of Comparative Rhetoric." *Rhetoric Society Quarterly* 39, no. 1 (2009): 353–79.

Swords, Alicia C. S., and Ronald L. Mize. *Consuming Mexican Labor: From the Bracero Program to NAFTA*. Toronto: University of Toronto Press, 2011.

Takenaga, Lara. "Why the Times Published a Photo of Drowned Migrants." *New York Times*, June 26, 2019. https://www.nytimes.com/2019/06/26/reader-center/rio-grande-migrants-photo.html.

Taylor-García, Daphne. *The Existence of the Mixed Race Damnés: Decolonialism, Class, Gender, Race*. Lanham, MD: Rowman and Littlefield, 2018.

Traux, Eileen. *We Built the Wall: How the US Keeps Out Asylum Seekers from Mexico, Central America and Beyond*. Translated by Diane Stockwell. New York: Verso, 2018.

Trump White House Archived. "06/26/19: President Trump Delivers a Statement upon Departure." YouTube, June 26, 2019. https://www.youtube.com/watch?v=eP2oJs FvpnY.

United States Border Patrol. *Border Patrol Strategic Plan 1994 and Beyond.* Homeland Security Digital Library, 1994. https://www.hsdl.org/?view&did=721845.

United States Customs and Border Protection. "Nationwide Enforcement Encounters: Title 8 Enforcement Actions and Title 42 Expulsions Fiscal Year 2020." U.S. Department of Homeland Security, March 27, 2023. https://www.cbp.gov/newsroom/stats /cbp-enforcement-statistics/title-8-and-title-42-statistics-fy2020#::text=Appre hensions%20refers%20to%20the%20physical,not%20result%20in%20an%20arrest.

————. "Southwest Border Unaccompanied Children FY 2014." U.S. Department of Homeland Security, October 13, 2016. https://www.cbp.gov/newsroom/stats/southwest -border-unaccompanied-children/fy-2014.

————. "Southwest Land Border Encounters." U.S. Department of Homeland Security, June 20, 2024. https://www.cbp.gov/newsroom/stats/southwest-land-border-encounters.

————. "U.S. Border Patrol Fiscal Year Southwest Border Sector Deaths (FY 1998–FY 2019)." U.S. Department of Homeland Security. August 16, 2021. https://www.cbp .gov/sites/default/files/assets/documents/2020-Jan/U.S.%20Border%20Patrol %20Fiscal%20Year%20Southwest%20Border%20Sector%20Deaths%20%28FY %201998%20-%20FY%202019%29_0.pdf.

United States Department of Justice Office of Public Affairs. "Attorney General Announces Zero-Tolerance Policy for Criminal Illegal Entry." April 6, 2018. https://www.justice .gov/opa/pr/attorney-general-announces-zero-tolerance-policy-criminal-illegal -entry.

United States House of Representatives. *Providing for Consideration of H.R. 6061, Secure Fence Act of 2006,* 109th Cong., 2nd sess. *Congressional Record* 152, pt. 13 (Bound ed. September 14, 2006): 18236–57. https://www.govinfo.gov/content/pkg/CRECB -2006-pt13/pdf/CRECB-2006-pt13-Pg18236.pdf.

United States Immigration and Naturalization Service. *Building a Comprehensive Southwest Border Enforcement Strategy.* Washington, DC: U.S. Department of Justice, 1996.

United States Office of the Inspector General. *Review of the Department of Justice's Planning and Implementation of Its Zero Tolerance Policy and Its Coordination with the Departments of Homeland Security and Health and Human Services.* Washington, DC: U.S. Department of Justice, 2021. https://oig.justice.gov/sites/default/files/reports/21–028 _0.pdf.

Urrea, Luis Alberto. *The Devil's Highway: A True Story.* New York: Little, Brown, 2004.

Vasconcelos, José. *The Cosmic Race.* Translated by Didier T. Jaén. Baltimore: Johns Hopkins University Press, 1979.

Vitanza, Victor J. "An After/word: Preparing to Meet the Faces That 'We' Will Have Met." In *Writing Histories of Rhetoric,* edited by Victor J. Vitanza, 217–57. Carbondale: Southern Illinois University Press, 1994.

————. *Negation, Subjectivity, and the History of Rhetoric.* Albany: SUNY Press, 1994.

Walker, Kenneth. *Climate Politics on the Border: Environmental Justice Rhetorics.* Tuscaloosa: University of Alabama Press, 2022.

Wallace, Karl R. "Topoi and the Problem of Invention." *Quarterly Journal of Speech* 58, no. 4 (1972): 387–95.

Wanzer-Serrano, Darrel. "Decolonial Rhetoric and a Future Yet-to-Become: A Loving Response." *Advances in the History of Rhetoric* 21, no. 3 (2018): 326–30.

Watts, Jonathan. "Driven by Fear: The Salvadorean Children Sent on the Perilous Journey to the US." *The Guardian*, August 29, 2015. https://www.theguardian.com/world/2015/aug/29/el-salvador-children-journey-us.

Weingarten, Debbie. "To All Parents Who Can Picture Themselves in Valeria and Her Dad." *The Guardian*, June 28, 2019. https://www.theguardian.com/us-news/2019/jun/28/migrant-father-daughter-drowned-valeria-parents.

Williams, Gareth. *Infrapolitical Passages: Global Turmoil, Narco-Accumulation, and the Post-Sovereign State*. New York: Fordham University Press, 2021.

———. *The Other Side of the Popular: Neoliberalism and Subalternity in Latin America*. Durham: Duke University Press, 2002.

Wolford, Lisa. "Afterword: Postcards from the Border Zone." In *Dangerous Border Crossers: The Artist Talks Back*, by Guillermo Gómez-Peña, 278–85. New York: Routledge, 2000.

Wong, Tom K. *The Politics of Immigration: Partisanship, Demographic Change, and American National Identity*. New York: Oxford University Press, 2017.

Yúdice, George. "Civil Society, Consumption, and Governmentality in an Age of Global Restructuring." *Social Text* 45 (1995): 1–25.

Zhao, Yunxia, Hamid Norouzi, Marzi Azarderakhsh, and Amir AghaKouchak. "Global Patterns of Hottest, Coldest, and Extreme Diurnal Variability on Earth." *Bulletin of the American Meteorological Society* 102, no. 4 (2021): E1672–81. https://journals.ametsoc.org/view/journals/bams/102/9/BAMS-D-20-0325.1.xml.

Žižek, Slavoj. "From Politics to Biopolitics . . . and Back." In *Biopolitics: A Reader*, edited by Timothy Campbell and Adam Sitze, 391–411. Durham: Duke University Press, 2013.

———. *In Defense of Lost Causes*. New York: Verso, 2008.

———. *The Puppet and the Dwarf: The Perverse Core of Christianity*. Cambridge: MIT Press, 2003.

Žižek, Slavoj, and Dianna Dillworth. "An Interview with Slavoj Zizek." *The Believer*, July 1, 2004. https://www.thebeliever.net/an-interview-with-slavoj-zizek/.

Index

RSA·STR

THE RSA SERIES IN TRANSDISCIPLINARY RHETORIC

www.ingramcontent.com/pod-product-compliance
Lightning Source LLC
Chambersburg PA
CBHW032145020426
42334CB00016B/1230